The N

Pollution H

GW00514717

Professor Chris Baines is an environmentalist who has always loved sharing nature with children. He was a founder of the Urban Wildlife movement in Britain, supported Sir David Attenborough as vice-chairman of the British Wildlife Appeal from 1985–1990, and is a member of the council of the Royal Society for Nature Conservation, the WWF-UK (World Wide Fund for Nature) and the Wildfowl and Wetlands Trust. He also has a long association with WATCH, and the Young Ornithologists Club.

Chris Baines works as an environmental adviser to central and local government, private industry, and to voluntary organisations too, and has a reputation for positive, practical ideas. He isn't a doom and gloom greenie.

His previous books are widely used in schools. *How to Make a Wildlife Garden* is a best-seller; *The Wild Side of Town* won the first Sir Peter Kent book prize in 1987, and Chris's four *Ecology Story Books* for young children are translated and sold all around the world.

Chris Baines has taken the conservation message onto TV. 'Bluetits and Bumblebees', 'Country File' and 'The Wild Side of Town' have helped thousands of viewers to enjoy the nature on their doorsteps. 'The Big E' was the first series to offer practical ideas to helping the environment, and 'The Ark' won the International Wildscreen award in 1987, when it was voted the best TV environmental series for young people.

NCVO – The Voice of the Voluntary Sector
Promoting the interests and effectiveness of voluntary organisations

NCVO was established in 1919 as the representative body for the voluntary sector. It is a membership-based organisation, including some 600 national voluntary organisations. Through its wide-ranging activities, NCVO is also in touch with thousands of other voluntary bodies and groups, and has formed close links with government departments, local authorities, the European Community, statutory and public bodies, and the business sector.

NCVO aims to promote the common interests of voluntary organisations; to provide, and encourage others to provide, a range of resources that will increase the effectiveness of voluntary organisations; and to extend the scope of the voluntary sector and identify new areas for action.

The latter role has led NCVO to set up new organisations over the years including Age Concern England, the Charities Aid Foundation, National Association of Citizens Advice Bureaux, and National Alliance of Women's Organisations.

National Council for Voluntary Organisations
26 Bedford Square, London WC1B 3HU
Tel 071–636 4066 Fax 071–436 3188

Bedford Square Press

Bedford Square Press is the publishing imprint of NCVO. It publishes books on a wide range of current social issues. Series published include Survival Handbooks, Community Action, Practical Guides, Directories, Reports, Organisation and Management, and Fundraising. If you would like to receive a copy of the latest catalogue, please write to: Marketing/Sales Manager, Bedford Square Press, 26 Bedford Square, London WC1B 3HU.

The New Pollution Handbook

An Action Guide to a Cleaner World

Bedford Square Press & **⊕WATCH**

Published by
Bedford Square Press of the
National Council for Voluntary organisations
26 Bedford Square, London WC1B 3HU

First published 1991

Typeset by AKM Associates (UK) Ltd, Southall, London
Printed and bound in Great Britain by
J.W. Arrowsmith, Bristol
This book is printed on recycled paper.

A catalogue record for this book is available from the British Library.

ISBN 0 7199 1263 6

Contents

Projects

Acknowledgements

Page: 23 Richmond Publishing Co Ltd and WATCH; 24 WATCH; 30–4 WATCH; 39–46 These illustrations are based on drawings from *The Pollution Handbook* by Richard Mabey (Penguin Books Ltd, 1974); 64–9 WATCH.

Foreword

When the nationwide surveys on which the original pollution handbook was based were launched in 1974, there were doubts about childrens' capacity to handle the technically complex and politically delicate subject of pollution. The results put all the sceptics to shame. Tens of thousands of young people sent in results which were exactingly researched and imaginatively presented, and whose accuracy was later confirmed during professional surveys. They knocked on the doors of dirty factories and pestered evasive planners. Above all they showed determination, and a belief that 'something should – and could – be done about it'.

Fifteen years on, as the green energies of the late 1980s flag a little, it is still young people who carry that optimistic torch. I feel privileged to introduce this completely new edition of the handbook, and hope that it will be as influential as the original. It could not be in better hands – nor children have a better champion – than Chris Baines.

Richard Mabey

Preface

In 1974, Richard Mabey wrote *The Pollution Handbook* – an important little book because it explained many different kinds of pollution problems, and the book was written specially for young people. Looking back now, it is depressing to see that almost all the environmental problems we now hear about every day were discussed in that book, and if anything, they are worse now than they were then. Some of the labels have changed – nobody was talking about 'acid rain' in 1974 – but the only real difference seems to be that we now know pollution can travel very great distances, and that some of the chemical pollution is having a damaging effect on a worldwide scale. Sixteen years ago there was very little talk of 'ozone layers' and 'Greenhouse effects'.

The laws to control pollution are slowly being strengthened all the time, and since the original pollution handbook was written, the European community in particular has raised our standards considerably. It is still true to say, though, that most cases of pollution – even the serious ones – go unpunished. Sometimes that is because it is difficult to prove who caused the problem, and sometimes new pollution control systems are so expensive that their swift introduction would put the polluter out of business.

One thing that really has changed dramatically in the past

few years is the interest that we all take in the environment generally, and pollution in particular. Now, more and more of us are doing something ourselves to try and make a difference. This is one area where the original handbook really did take the lead, because it was a practical guide to action. What is more, it used the projects that young people were already involved in to show just what we could do, firstly to measure pollution, and then to help reduce it. That principle has been the backbone of WATCH ever since. The young members of WATCH have really become world leaders when it comes to uniting scientific study with environmental action. The WATCH projects are taken very seriously by central and local government, and I know of conservation groups as far afield as New York, the Himalayas, the Indian Ocean, the Soviet Union and Equador who use them as a means of measuring their own local environment. Over the years, hundreds of thousands of young people have had a great deal of fun, splashing around in streams, gathering acid rain, recycling cans, and generally getting to grips with the environment on their doorstep: their example has shamed some grown-ups, and inspired others, as the WATCH projects go from strength to strength. Every year more than 10,000 WATCH members pour bags of energy and enthusiasm into the latest national WATCH project, and every year their collective results help persuade the decision-makers to act. In the past, most young environmentalists worked as members of a club. More and more people are joining local WATCH clubs each year, but lots of the pollution monitoring and practical action can be done on your own or with a friend, or with the family.

This book should provide the background information needed to understand where pollution comes from, how you can spot it and measure it safely, and how we can all do much more to help the earth become a cleaner, healthier place for people and wildlife to share.

Chris Baines

Thanks

I would like to thank Richard Mabey, for encouraging me to follow in his footsteps. I hope this book inspires young people in the same way that his original did.

BT has made the book possible through its generous sponsorship. It is an appropriate supporter, since the telephone and the fax machine save me, and millions of others, a great many polluting journeys every week.

WATCH, the Junior Section of the RSNC Wildlife Trusts Partnership, deserves my thanks, since it provided much of the background data, and its inspiring projects over the years have introduced so many young people to positive conservation. Wayne Talbot in particular has given solid support and encouragement.

WATCH is only as good as its local groups, and the hundreds of WATCH leaders up and down the country deserve a special mention, for leading hundreds of thousands of children out into the environment, and managing through their enthusiasm, technical knowledge and caring common sense, to make environmental study great fun.

It is the children themselves who have done the work – trekking out to the Acid Drops collection point, night after night, filling sacks with recyclable cans, and splashing through streams and ponds in search of indicator species – so of course we all owe *them* a vote of thanks.

And last, but by no means least, I feel we should thank the wild life that shares the planet with us. From the flocks of wading birds on our tidal estuaries, to the humble rat-tailed maggots in our murky ponds; from the leafless trees of our acidified forests, to the starlings and seagulls that gobble up our garbage; we owe them all a great debt of gratitude. The wild plants and animals are giving up their lives to satisfy our greed – and all of them are screaming the same clear message. Pollution is a killer. Already it is killing many of *them*, and unless we learn that lesson, and begin the urgent task of helping the earth get better, then there can be no doubt that pollution will destroy *us* too.

About
This Book

It's pretty obvious that pollution is likely to get worse as the world's population rises, and more people crowd together in towns. There is simply not enough space for nature to do her basic clean-up job. The more complicated convenience products often lead to the most waste and the most serious chemical pollution, and our use of energy is perhaps the greatest single source of serious pollution.

It's also obvious that however clever we continue to be at disguising pollution problems – sweeping them under the carpet, or pumping them out of sight – they don't really go away. The earth now seems a very small place. Our wasteful way of life affects the environment directly, even on the far side of the globe.

The problems are of our own making. It is the way we live that creates pollution, and as the people of the under-developed world begin to demand more of the luxurious wasteful lifestyle we in the industrialised West enjoy, pollution is in danger of destroying whole areas of the earth.

The problems are immense – but they are all created by people like us. The pessimists throw up their hands in despair, and cry that greedy people will never change! On the other hand, the optimists say that if individuals created the problem, individuals should be able to solve them.

This is an optimist's guide to pollution, which shows that there are four basic ways in which each of us can help turn the tide of pollution.

Turning the tide

We need to be much more alert to the first signs. So many serious pollution problems can be prevented if they're spotted in time – so we need far more pollution spotters – people who can keep an eye out for the tell-tale signs that mean the environment's being poisoned. This book will tell you where to look, and what to look for, and who the people are who can do something with the information.

There is also a need to know much more about the kinds and quantities of pollution. Of course it's possible to do that job with expensive equipment, operated by highly skilled scientists – but actually most of us can tell a bad smell from a sweet perfume, or a dead river from a healthy one. Thanks to the work of WATCH, you will find several projects in this book that will enable you to make a much cleverer, more scientific assessment of pollution than that.

Once you've measured the pollution problem, you'll want to try and stop it. Often you'll need help. None of us can take on the manager of a power station or a chemical works single handed, and you need to be pretty brave even to dare to mention the smoke, or the noise pollution pouring out of big sister's old banger – but there are some kinds of pollution that you *can* help to clean up, and this book will tell you how.

Finally, and perhaps most exciting of all, we all need to produce less pollution in the first place – and that generally means being less wasteful, and making use of things that would otherwise get thrown away. The three Rs are very easy to remember:

- *Refuse* If you don't need the packaging or the car-ride to school or the extra warmth of the central heating – say no and *reduce pollution.*
- *Re-use* – anything you can. So many things are thrown away just because we're bored with them, or we've grown out of them. If you don't need it anymore – pass it on to someone who does, and *reduce pollution.*
- *Recycle* When the first life of any of your possessions is over, whether it's a pop-bottle or a piece of furniture, if you can't re-use it as it is, then find a way of re-cycling the materials it's made of. That way you'll *reduce pollution,* save on raw materials and often save on the energy used in manufacturing, too.

1 The Overloaded System

There is plenty of waste in the natural world, but most of the time nature manages to deal with it successfully.

When the leaves fall from the trees in autumn, they may blow around, and block up the gutters for a week or two, but when they eventually come to rest, earthworms soon begin to pull them down into the earth. A whole range of different animals begin to eat them, fungal spores germinate and the leaves begin to rot. Within a few months, even in the relatively cold wet climate of Britain, the leaves will be broken down to become a part of the soil, and to help the trees grow even more.

When an animal dies, then the same thing happens. If poor unfortunate hedgehogs get run over, they don't lie around, polluting the environment for long, because other species quickly move in to clear up the mess! Magpies and crows have become very skilled at hopping around on the hard-shoulder, nipping out into the road between cars, and starting the natural process of pollution control by pecking up the pieces.

This kind of natural waste only turns into a pollution problem if the natural 'clean-up' systems can't cope. In nature that can happen, but not very often. If those autumn leaves fall into a pond, then most of the organisms that might chew them up and rot them down can't survive under water, so it takes much longer for the leaves to decompose. While it's happening, some of the animals in the pond may be poisoned by the chemicals the leaves turn into, so you could say this is a natural form of pollution.

When a flock of starlings flies in to roost night after night in the same group of trees, then the build-up of their droppings can foul the area, killing the plants on the woodland floor, and producing a very smelly, polluted place.

Most of the time, though, the waste products of nature are dealt with long before they become a pollution problem. Most of the serious pollution in the world is caused by humans. People have always had a nasty habit of 'throwing things away', and although nature can cope with some of our waste, very often we overload the system, and our waste becomes a problem.

Most of the natural processes for dealing with waste work best in warm, damp, airy conditions. That's the kind of environment the vital organisms of decay need. If it gets too wet, for instance, as it would be in the pond, then there is a shortage of air, and few of the organisms can survive.

Peat bogs are too wet for the natural process of decay, and so peat-digging often reveals perfectly preserved specimens. For instance, trees thousands of years old lie buried there, perfect right down to the last leaf. There is too much water and not enough air for organisms of decay to survive in the peat, and nothing rots down. Over the years, all kinds of things have been dug out of peat in almost perfect condition – things like roman sandals and pieces of ancient clothing, which would have rotted away if they had fallen onto drier ground. Even dead bodies turn up from time to time. 'Pete Marsh' was an ancient Britain, killed over a thousand years ago, and thrown into the bog, where he was preserved right up to the day when a peat digger uncovered him again.

In the frozen wastelands of northern Russia, and elsewhere

in the Polar ice-cap, whole specimens of prehistoric woolly mammoths have been found, perfectly preserved and 'fresh' enough to eat, although they have been extinct for thousands of years. Here, the problem for the organisms of decay isn't just lack of air – it's the *cold*. The whole of the polar region is like a giant deep-freeze, and while the woolly mammoths stay frozen they don't rot down. As soon as they're dug up and thawed out, they start to decay, and quickly turn into smelly mammoths.

In the hot deserts of the Wild West, the heroes of the cowboy films always seem to gallop past the dusty remains of a dead cow at some point in the story. The rate of decay in the desert is very slow because it's too *dry* for most of the natural organisms of decay to do their job, so the poor old 'steer' might take years to rot away.

Nature's pollution control systems are very, very efficient. If they weren't, our woods would be filled to the tree-tops with fallen leaves, our motorways would be piled high with squashed hedgehogs, and everywhere would be very smelly, and very messy. In fact, natural pollution is very rare.

How people produce pollution

We create pollution in a number of ways. First, we overload the natural processes of decay. We pile up so much rubbish, or pump so much sewage into the rivers, that the natural organisms of decay just can't cope. That's partly a problem that comes from living together in large numbers, and concentrating all our waste in small areas.

The second way we create pollution is by putting things into the environment that actually kill the helpful natural organisms. Oil on the surface of a lake, for instance, will cut off the oxygen so the fish and the water creatures die. Chemicals may blow out of a factory chimney, be picked up by the rain, and fall onto plants and animals hundreds of miles away, and may poison them. Poisonous waste may be taken out to sea in ships, and dumped on the sea-bed – killing the shellfish and other creatures that normally help to clean things up.

We also create pollution because we throw away things on which the natural process of decay simply don't work. They won't rot down, and nothing will eat them, so they're *non-biodegradable*. Of course, there's nothing new in that. The reason we know so much about ancient civilisations, like the Greeks and Romans, is because they 'polluted' their surroundings with broken pots, metal ornaments, and other 'non-biodegradable' bits and pieces that have never rotted down.

Nowadays most of *our* rubbish is rather less glamorous than a Grecian urn or a roman sword – it's plastic bottles, glass jam-jars and polystyrene cups – but just like the ancient archaeological treasures, nature doesn't rot them down. A walk along the tide-line of the seashore, or a hunt in a roadside hedge-bottom will soon show you the kind of treasures we're leaving behind.

I wonder if the British Museum is planning a 'rubbish room' for displaying the old car-tyres and crisp-packets of the twentieth century.

What can we do?

Since we are the people who create most of the pollution in the world, it seems pretty obvious that we need to do as much as we can to put it right. Some of the modern pollution problems may seem far too remote for us to help as individuals. It's not easy to see immediately how we can clean up the oceans or stop acid rain single-handed.

In fact, though, we *can* do a great deal to help, but it needs a serious commitment from everyone. I'm sure you're the greenest of green, but you need to take a bit of time off, in between your trips to the bottle-bank, your waste-paper collections, and your sessions behind the counter at the local second-hand shop, to pester everybody else to do their bit.

Keep on asking people why they don't seem to care. Why do they travel by car when they could take the train? Why do they spray their gardens with pesticides, and tip any left-over chemicals straight down the drain? Why don't they draught-proof the doors and windows properly, and save energy. Already there are lots of people doing lots to help – but there are many more who just don't seem to think it's worth bothering. You've got to persuade them that it is.

2 The Growth of Pollution

There has been life on earth for millions of years. Throughout all that time, nature has maintained a healthy balance. It is only in the past few hundred years that mankind has managed to cause serious damage to the environment. From the time when we began to dominate nature, we have exploited the natural resources of the earth, and as we have become more and more wasteful, one of the problems we have caused is pollution.

We know from the studies of archaeologists, the scientists who dig around and uncover clues to the ancient past, that problems started as soon as people stopped wandering, and began to settle. They created rubbish tips. It is the fragments of bone, the broken pots and the discarded tools, that tell us so much about the way the prehistoric people lived. We know, for instance, that they were great recyclers. They used empty sea-shells as containers, animal's bones as tools and jewellery, and skins from the animals they ate, to make their clothes. Nevertheless, the area around their cave entrance or their shelter would have quickly become littered with waste bits and pieces. You can find the same kind of mild pollution around a fox's lair today.

When people began to gather together in towns the waste

problem grew much worse. The streets of medieval Britain must have been disgusting. Every kind of waste was thrown out of doors and windows. The people built gutters down the middle of the roads to carry the worst of the pollution away into the nearest stream, and there were plenty of scavengers around to eat the rest. These included rats, dogs, cats, crows, and even red kites, birds which are very rare in Britain today. Despite the stench, and the risk of disease, in those days polluters had one great advantage over us. Almost everything they threw away was a natural material, and it would rot down quite quickly.

That was still true until about 200 years ago. Then along came the industrial revolution. In fact it began in Britain. Suddenly people were crowded together in fast-growing towns and cities. That meant the old ways of getting rid of waste had to change. The streets and streams just couldn't cope with such huge concentrations of waste, so systems were developed to take away the pollution each individual family produced. Usually it ended up dumped in the countryside beyond the edge of town. City rubbish tips were invented, to take the waste ash from millions of open fires, and all the other rubbish that people produced. Nowadays those old tips are popular places for 'treasure-hunters' to dig for old glass pop-bottles, clay pipes and any other century-old junk that hasn't rotted away.

Sewage

Before the industrial revolution, sewage didn't really exist. Almost everybody had an earth-closet, a kind of primitive lavatory that was simply a shed in the garden or the back yard, with a wooden seat over a deep hole in the ground. In fact some people had two- or three-seater closets; quite a strange place to go for a quiet chat. Earth closets were OK for gardens out in the countryside, but they weren't really suitable for the tightly-packed streets of the big new industrial cities. At first, the 'human manure' was collected on a regular basis, and taken out to spread as fertilizer on the fields beyond the town; recycling on a grand scale. Manchester Council even built a special railway, just to carry the tons of 'night-soil' that the city's residents produced each day, and the lucky people with the smelly job of shovelling up the sewage were known affectionately (but not too affectionately) as the 'Midnight Angels'. In China, even today, night soil is a very important source of fertilizer. That helps to explain how that enormous overcrowded country manages to feed almost one-fifth of the world's population.

The flushing lavatory couldn't be introduced until people in towns had access to piped water, and that only started towards the end of the last century – not much more than a hundred years ago. Then, the 'human manure' could be washed away down pipes and sewers, to be dealt with somewhere else. The Midnight Angels were out of a job. Originally, most of this raw liquid sewage was piped straight into a river, or the sea, and surprisingly, about a fifth of it is still dumped there, untreated, even today. Even where there is a sewage treatment works, if often has a kind of safety valve overflow system built in, to take the extra amounts of sewage and storm water that flow down the sewers after heavy rain. When the system overflows, raw sewage usually ends up decorating the river banks or being washed up on the beach somewhere downstream.

If water-closets – WCs – had simply been used for the 'human manure' they were designed to take, pollution wouldn't have been much of a problem, but a nice convenient 'convenience' in the house, that will flush almost any waste product 'out of sight and out of mind' is too tempting for most of us. As we have become more and more wasteful, the variety of things we have poured down the sewers has increased alarmingly, and now a combination of liquid chemicals and solid bits and pieces is preventing sewage treatment from working properly. It's amazing how many bits of rubber and plastic are flushed away each day, and when they eventually arrive at the sewage works, they clog up the holes in the water sprinklers, get tangled up round the moving parts, and play havoc with the whole sewage treatment system. Some of the chemicals are simply poisonous – things like weedkillers, bleaches, medicines and paint. Sewage works can't deal with them, but worse than that, they actually kill off the natural organisms – the bacteria and algae – that do most of the work of sewage treatment.

The damage done by some chemicals is less obvious, but just as bad. Most of our washing powders and detergents contain phosphates, for instance. Phosphates help to make the products work better, but when we empty the washing machine or the dishwasher, or drive through the car-wash, those phosphates pour down the drains, into the sewers, and unaffected by the sewage works, they eventually end up in a river or the sea. There, they help the green slimey algae to grow like mad, and when the algae die, and start to rot down, they use up the oxygen in the water, and the wildlife dies. Now, at last, the manufacturers are starting to sell detergents without phosphate, and slowly this particular kind of pollution should be reduced.

Stacks of trouble

Our clever great-grandfathers used underground sewage pipes to take water pollution away, and dump it in the environment. They used tall chimney-stacks to do the same with the air pollution from millions of coal fires, factories and furnaces. Most of the time the system did them proud. The smoke puffed out of the top of the chimneys and was blown away on the wind. When the wind didn't blow, or the night air was particularly cold, the smoke just hung around the buildings, and built up into dense fog so thick you couldn't see across the street, and so chokingly polluting that thousands of people were killed each year, and millions more suffered with breathing problems and bronchitis. The very thickest fogs were known as 'pea-soupers' – and if you've seen how thick and yellowish-green a good old fashioned pea-soup looks, you'll know just what a serious pollution problem the town fogs were. They were common for a hundred years or more, from the middle of the last century to the middle of this. Throughout that time, our towns and cities were too polluted for many species of wildlife to survive. One or two adapted. Over a few generations they changed their colour, from the light colours that camouflaged them against a clean background, they became darker and darker, keeping pace with the blackening walls and trees as these became stained by the smoke and soot. This process, known as melanism, is particularly obvious in a species of moth, the pepper moth, which stayed almost white in unpolluted rural areas, but became black in the grimey industrial cities. Many other species, including bluetits and sparrows, became darker generation by generation too. Now the worst of the 'pea-soupers' have passed, these melanistic species will gradually become lighter in colour again.

About 40 years ago, the government of the day decided something must be done about city air pollution. The Clean Air Act 1956 was passed, and people were forced to control the smoke. Many were told they could no longer burn coal in their homes, so quite rapidly they switched to coke, oil, gas or electricity. Factories were forced to reduce the effect of their smoke, too. Most of them responded by building taller chimneys, to make sure the smoke was blown away more effectively. The 'smokeless' fuels certainly seemed to do the trick, and the town fogs died out, but really all that had happened was that once again the pollution had been pushed a bit further away – out of sight and out of mind. The smokeless coke, which replaced the smoky coal, was made by taking most of the polluting chemicals out before it was delivered. Town gas was one of the products, but there was also a great deal of particularly nasty chemical waste which created some of the very worst concentrations of water and air pollution we've ever produced. In fact, smokeless fuel works are still amongst our worst polluters.

Electricity became more and more popular. It seemed such a spotlessly clean source of energy, but of course it was generated by burning coal, gas or oil in power stations out in the countryside, and pushing all the smoke up one big chimney instead of hundreds of little ones. The resulting pollution was actually just as bad. The taller chimneys, on the factories, the furnaces and the power stations themselves, certainly lifted the cloud of smoke much higher, and allowed the wind to blow it much further, but eventually the chemicals in the smoke still fell to earth, and we know that they helped cause the problem known as *acid rain.* As our moths and bluetits, and our smoke-blackened town-hall walls were all becoming cleaner and brighter again, the acids in our smoke were polluting streams and rivers a thousand or more miles away in Sweden, Norway, North Germany and beyond – killing fish, and rapidly destroying the forests of Northern Europe, too.

Wrapping up the problem

In the past 40 years, we have become more and more wasteful. Packaging, and particularly plastic wrapping, has increased dramatically as we have changed our shopping habits from buying fresh food daily at the corner shop or the market stall, to a weekly or fortnightly expedition to the supermarket. Almost all of that packaging is used once and then thrown away – either to litter the streets or to fill a hole in the ground somewhere out in the countryside.

Scientific pollution

Chemicals are the other modern evil. Thousands of new chemicals have been invented, from paints and weedkillers to preservatives and hair sprays. We all use them every day, and we use most of them without much care. When we have some chemical left over we just dump it, and manufacturers sometimes do the same. Complex and dangerous wastes are often simply carted away and dumped at sea, or burned, and turned into air-polluting clouds of smoke and poisonous ash. Some of the deadliest poisons ever produced result from burning chemical waste, and the seas around our coast are becoming increasingly sick, as the chemicals we dump at sea poison first the plants, then the tiny sea creatures, and eventually the fish, the birds and the mammals.

We now know that the pollution we dump in the sea or in the air can travel huge distances. Polar bears at the North Pole, and penguins at the South, contain traces of poisonous chemicals in their bodies which have travelled tens of thousands of miles from the industrialised countries of the world. No doubt they are picked up by migratory fish and birds, or simply washed along in the ocean's currents. Some of the chemicals scientists have invented for our convenience have escaped into the atmosphere, and are now polluting the air many miles above us. The most well-known examples are a range of chemicals, called *chloro-flouro carbons* (CFCs). These gases are used in refrigerators, to provide the 'pssshh' in aerosols, and to blow the bubbles into polystyrene foam. When they rise up into the atmosphere, scientists now tell us that they destroy ozone – a natural gas which helps form a protective layer around the earth. As the ozone layer gets thinner, more of the sun's powerful burning rays are able to penetrate down to earth, causing damage to plants and animals, and increasing the risk of skin-cancer for humans.

Global Greenhouse

Fuel burning has always been a cause of air pollution. Back in the iron-age, when people lived in stone huts and cooked over a wood-fire in the middle of the room, they must have lived with their eyes permanently watering from the smoke, as it swirled around before finally leaking out through a hole in the thatched roof. The gases of our industrial cities spread a black cloud of pollution over the rooftops, and the power stations have helped create acid rain.

The fuel we burn for transport is creating the most recent pollution boom. The internal combustion engine burns fuel oil – usually either diesel or petrol, although in Brazil they now burn alcohol distilled from cane-sugar. As it burns, very inefficiently, it gives off energy to drive the pistons and turn the engine, but it also produces exhaust gases – air pollution. Some of the chemical fumes are quite similar to the polluting gases from power stations and factory chimneys, and there is one group of polluting gases that we have only just begun to understand. These are the carbon gases – particularly carbon dioxide and carbon monoxide. They are produced by burning the carbon in oil, or any of the other carbon fuels – coal, natural gas, even wood or straw. They've always been present in the atmosphere – indeed carbon dioxide is essential to life on earth. Without it green plants can't take the sun's energy and create the new material that we all depend on. The problem is the amount of the carbon dioxide that we're now pouring out into the atmosphere. We've only been burning fossil fuels for about 200 years, but we do burn them at a dramatic rate. We get a great deal of the energy used around the world by burning oil, coal or gas. The resulting carbon gases are building up, high in the atmosphere, and just as the ozone layer keeps out some of the sun's power, the carbon gases keep in the heat that is building up around the surface of the earth. For this reason they are known as the green-house gases, and they cause the greenhouse effect. As we convert more and more carbon into carbon dioxide, carbon monoxide, methane and other greenhouse gases, they pollute the whole earth in a very frightening way. No one knows just how life on earth will adapt, but scientists do agree that the greenhouse effect is increasing at an alarmingly rapid rate, that the temperature of the earth's atmosphere is rising, and that we are likely to see changes in climate and sea level within our lifetime.

As we enjoy the short-term convenience of our cars and lorries, the luxury of central heating, and the manufactured products of our modern industries, we are helping to create pollution problems on a scale that nobody expected, and at present pollution at almost every level is getting worse. There is an urgent need for all of us to change our ways.

3 Pinpointing Pollution

It is amazing how many people seem to live alongside serious pollution, and never even notice. Of course, there are professional people whose job it is to look for pollution problems. They're called *environmental health officers*, and they work for local councils. You can find the council's telephone number in the phone book and if you ring, they'll put you through to the Environmental Health Department. Environmental health officers are highly trained and committed to cleaning up our surroundings, but it's pretty obvious that in most places, they're not able to cope on their own. They need our help.

Over the past 15 years, tens of thousands of young people have worked through projects organised by WATCH, to carry out surveys in their neighbourhood, measuring pollution levels in the local streams and rivers, or in the air itself. These projects – the clean rivers project, the Lichen Count, Acid Drops and the Ozone Project – are described later in the book, and there is certainly a need to keep on carrying out this kind of work, but there are simpler things that everyone of us can do immediately.

Become a pollution watch-dog

The environment needs lots more *watch-dogs* – so from now on use your eyes to spot problems, and remember, your nose can sometimes sniff out pollution before you actually see it. If you do find something you think is pollution, contact the council's environmental health officers. They may know about it already, but even if they do, at least they'll know that someone else out there is as concerned as they are – and you might just alert them to a problem they hadn't heard about.

Some of the evidence of pollution is very obvious if you start looking for it. What you need to do is to adopt a patch of your local neighbourhood. It might be the route you follow to school, or the area you can see from your bedroom window.

It's a very good idea to join up with a friend right from the start. Apart from the obvious advantage of doubling the eyes and noses involved, it means that if you do spot a pollution problem, and particularly if you catch someone red-handed, dumping rubbish, for instance, or pouring used engine oil down a drain – then you will have two witnesses instead of one.

To do the job thoroughly you'll probably need to poke around in the quieter corners of your 'pollution prevention patch'. You're more likely to find problems 'round the back of the factory' or 'over the garden fence', where people don't often go. It is important not to trespass onto private land. If you're suspicious, call the environmental health officers because they have the power to go in and inspect. But creeping around on your own, even in the public areas, can be a bit scary, especially if you happen to spot a polluter in action. These people are obviously not environmentally friendly, so they're not very likely to be 'watch-dog friendly' either, and you may be glad of a partner. If you do spot pollution taking place, don't try to tackle the polluter yourself. Make a note of the details, and report them to the Environmental Health Officer.

Where there's smoke there's pollution

Chimneys are the simplest place to start looking for pollution. They're nice and tall, and easy to see. They are designed to take smoke and gases and carry them up into the air, so that they blow away in the breeze. Unfortunately, the smoke doesn't just disappear. Chimneys are built much taller now than they used to be. In the days when they were shorter, the smoke often didn't blow away at all. Instead it used to hang around in the air, and in industrial towns this produced very bad, and very obvious pollution. Now, with taller chimneys, industrial smoke is blown out of the town, but eventually the tiny particles of soot, and the chemicals in the smoke, fall back to the ground – so the people and the wildlife somewhere else suffer from our pollution.

The amount and the type of waste smoke and gases that any particular company is allowed to blow out into the air is decided by the local council, and again it is the environmental health officer who decides if a polluter is breaking the law.

Quite often, though, the clouds of smoke will only appear for a short time, when something especially nasty is being burned, and some of the craftiest polluters will choose a time to get rid of their problem when they think nobody is watching. That may be after dark, when it's difficult to spot, though the smell might still give them away.

The other favourite time for bad cases for polluting smoke is at weekends, when the officials at the town hall are less likely to be around. If you spot a chimney churning out clouds of smelly or dirty-looking smoke on a Sunday morning, phone the environmental health officer anyway. You may be greeted by an ansaphone, but nowadays many councils have someone on duty every day of the week. If you have to leave a message, make sure you tell them who you are, and how you can be contacted – giving your phone number or address; when and where you saw the polluting smoke and what it looked like –

especially the colour. If there was someone else with you who saw the same thing, let the council know there's a second witness.

Reporting pollution coming out of chimneys is easy. Factories, hospitals and power stations can't go away and hide – but they're not the only source of smoky pollution. A lot of the problem now comes from motor vehicles. Most of the time the exhaust fumes aren't visible, so although there are ways of measuring the general levels of traffic pollution, it's not always easy to spot which of the cars, lorries and buses are causing the worst problem. Sometimes, though, especially with big diesel engine – buses, lorries and trains – you do actually see the pollution pouring out of the exhaust pipe in a cloud of black smoke. That's a sign that the vehicle isn't running efficiently, and although the smoke may not be the most poisonous of the gases produced, it probably does mean that the people who own the lorry are breaking the pollution control laws and that there are other poisonous gases being released, too.

One good thing about polluting vehicles is that they all carry licence plates, with their own individual number on them, so if you can still read the number plate through the cloud of black smoke, it's possible for the police to trace the owner, and do something about getting the problem cleaned up.

Action

- Find out the telephone number of the council's Environmental Health Office.
- Join a friend, and become a pollution spotter.
- Choose a local pollution patch, and inspect it regularly for signs of pollution.

Ozone Project

Ozone is a gas. It's part of the air around us. It is produced naturally, from oxygen, and as everybody knows, it helps form a layer high up in the air – 40 km above the surface of the earth. That 'ozone layer' helps protect us all from the power of the sun, but scientists have shown that this protection is getting very thin. The high-level ozone is being damaged by a whole range of man-made pollution, and especially by chemicals called CFCs (Chloro-fluro carbons). Lots of us have stopped using products with CFCs in them – aerosol sprays, polystyrene foam and old-fashioned refrigerators, for instance – as a way of helping protect the ozone layer. 'Ozone friendly' is now printed on many of the products in supermarkets.

High up there above the earth, ozone is a good gas, so it's very confusing to be told that ozone is also bad for the environment. Down here at ground level, too much ozone can cause all kinds of problems. It gives some people breathing difficulties – so much so that in some parts of the world, schools are closed and children are kept indoors when there's an ozone warning on the radio. Ozone can also damage plants and wildlife.

The ground level ozone pollution problem is caused when other polluting gases – particularly those from traffic and power stations – are affected by sunshine. This kind of chemical smog is especially bad in sunny cities with a traffic problem. Rome, Athens and Los Angeles each suffer from serious ozone pollution.

It is possible to measure the amount of ozone in the air using very expensive electronic machines, and the government collects this information at a few points around the country. Now there is another way of measuring the problem, too. WATCH has produced an ozone project pack, to help collect local ozone data. In its first year, over 10,000 pollution WATCH dogs bought an ozone pack. Scientists can use the records from all these individual samples to find out how the pollution level compares in different places, and in different weather conditions.

The basic equipment for the survey isn't a big expensive computer – it's a little green plant. In fact, it's two very special kinds of plants. Many species of plants are damaged by ozone pollution, but scientists have discovered that one type in particular produces spots on its leaves if the pollution is bad. The worse the pollution, the more spots there are, and the more rapidly the leaves die.

The WATCH ozone survey involves growing seedlings of the test plant – a particular variety of the tobacco plant 'Nicotiana tobacum'. It seems crazy to grow tobacco in order to test for air pollution, but it really does work. The variety that suffers from spots is called 'Nicotiana tobacum cultivar Bel-W3'. Another variety, called 'Nicotiana tobacum cultivar Bel-B' doesn't get spots on its leaves, except in highest levels of pollution – so the experiment is simple. You need to grow healthy seedlings of the two different kinds of tobacco plant – and you must be careful not to mix up the labels because they look identical at first. Once they're growing well, plant them side by side, in the area you want to test for ozone pollution. Perhaps you might choose two places – the front garden, close to the traffic, and the back garden away from the traffic.

If you're doing the experiment on your own, you can simply watch, to see whether the Bel-W3 seedlings turn spotty, and the test card will give you an idea of how bad the pollution is. Of course, if both kinds of seedlings turn spotty, it probably means they're suffering from other problems, and you can't be sure the ozone's to blame.

For the National WATCH survey, it was very important for the scientists to be able to compare results, so experimenters all over the country had to start their leaf watching on the same day.

The two packets of seed had to be sown at the same time, and kept indoors, with plenty of light and warmth – but no direct sunlight – for the first eight weeks. As they grew they needed to be transplanted into their own individual pots. In week eight, the pots were moved outside to toughen up the little plants, and in week nine they were planted in the test site. Then each Wednesday, for the following three weeks, the leaves were 'observed' and their spottiness was checked against the test card. At the end of the third week, the measurements were sent off to WATCH.

When the ozone pollution was bad – in very sunny weather – the spots on the leaves were creamy coloured and they developed quickly. In duller weather, the pollution leaves were not so bad, and then, if there was still an ozone problem, the spots that formed were brown.

By collecting so many test-samples from so many different places, the scientists were able to show just how serious the ozone pollution was, and how it varied with the weather.

Reducing the ozone problem

To reduce the problems of the ground-level ozone pollution, we need to use cars less, and to have them fitted with a kind of filter, called a catalytic converter. The exhaust gases blow through this, and most of the pollution that would otherwise turn into ozone is cleaned up or converted to less harmful gases.

The WATCH experiment is planned to run for at least

two summers – partly to see if there is a drop in ozone pollution as more and more cars are fitted with catalytic converters. In many other countries in Europe and North America, cars are already 'cleaned up', and ozone pollution problems have been reduced.

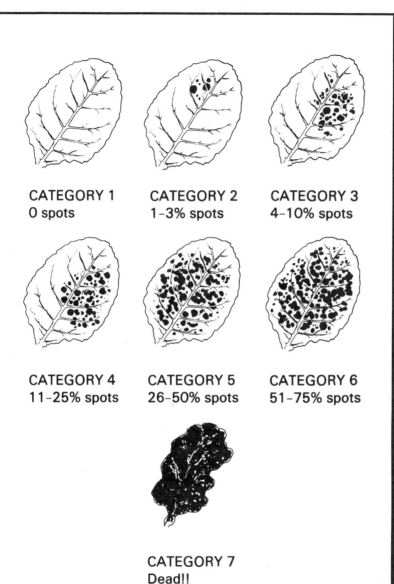

CATEGORY 1
0 spots

CATEGORY 2
1-3% spots

CATEGORY 3
4-10% spots

CATEGORY 4
11-25% spots

CATEGORY 5
26-50% spots

CATEGORY 6
51-75% spots

CATEGORY 7
Dead!!

Use less energy for transport.
The diagram shows how far you can travel
using a gallon of fuel on different types of
transport.

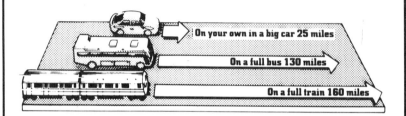

On your own in a big car 25 miles

On a full bus 130 miles

On a full train 160 miles

Don't use polluting products.

If everyone followed
these easy steps
there would be much
less pollution and
wasted energy.

Cars can be fitted
with catalytic
converters. These
reduce the polluting
gases that cause
ground level ozone
and acid rain. Does
your car have one?

Use only CFC free aerosols.

Ozone Project – summary

What you're measuring

Ozone gas down at traffic level.

What you need

Plant pots.
Compost.
Seeds of the two special indicator plants:
Nicotiana tobacum Bel-W3 and Nicotiana tobacum Bel-B.

Where to sample

Two sites where you can look after your indicator plants:
one near a busy road, and one well away from the traffic.

When to sample

This is a spring and summer project, and you'll need three
months to grow the seedlings and measure ozone levels.

How the project can help fight pollution locally

Your indicator plants will show how good or bad ozone
pollution levels are. Evidence of high ozone levels can help
persuade the local council to reduce traffic levels.

Importance of the National WATCH project

Lots of results from young pollution monitors around the country have shown how serious the levels of ozone pollution are, and which kind of places have the worst problem. This information can help with better planning of traffic, and encourage a move from car and lorry transport, to bus and rail transport as a means of reducing pollution.

Acid Drops Project

Some of the chemicals in the smoke from factories, coal fires, power stations, and vehicle exhaust pipes can be dissolved in rain water, making it more acid. That acid rain can damage the environment by wearing away the stone work of old buildings, polluting lakes and rivers and poisoning trees.

Scientists measure how acid things are, and give them a score called a pH (pronounced pea-aitch) number. The most acid things score pH0. and at the other end of the scale, the most alkaline things score pH14. Anything that is neither acid nor alkaline is called 'neutral' and scores pH7. Most things are either acid or alkaline. Here are typical scores for some common things around the house.

pH   2.0 – lemon juice   – acid
pH   2.0 – vinegar   – acid
pH   3.0 – apples   – acid
pH   6.5 – milk   – almost neutral
pH   8.0 – baking soda   – slightly alkaline
pH   8.1 – sea water   – alkaline
pH 10.5 – milk of magnesia   – alkaline
pH 11.0 – ammonia   – alkaline

Normal rain is slightly acid – pH 5.6. By using a special kind of paper, it is possible to measure how acid or alkaline your own rain water is.

If you don't have the full WATCH acid drops kit, then you will need to buy some acid testing papers or special sticks that change colour in acids and alkalis. When you dip one of them in the rain-water, and then match it against a colour chart, that will tell you the pH of the water.

Collecting the rain

You need to collect your samples for testing in such a way that they don't get dirty. If you were just to put a dish on the ground, rain would splash all around the outside, and soil might 'bounce' up and pollute the sample. You need to collect your sample out in the open, away from the drips off trees and buildings, and at least 1 metre above ground level.

How to make a rainwater collecting station

You need a large plastic pop-bottle, a stout straight bamboo cane or a stake at least 1.5 metres long, clean polythene bags, and three rubber bands.

- Drive the stake into the ground, in a good, open part of the garden.
- Cut the bottom off the bottle, and then turn the bottomless bottle upside down, so that the new hole is at the top.
- Put a polythene bag inside the bottle, and fold it over the rim, so it will catch the rain-water. Hold it in place with an elastic band.
- Fix the upside-down bottomless bottle to the top of the stake with the other rubber bands. (See figures 1-5.)

Use a clean polythene bag each day, taking away the old bag, containing any rain-water or snow that you've collected, and seal the bag until you're ready to test it.

Try and collect your sample at the same time each day, and if you really want to do a thorough job, use a compass each day and make a note of which direction the wind is blowing *from*. Also look at the weather report on TV, and find out which way the wind has been blowing across your area. Most of the time, the wind in Britain blows from the South West towards the North East – from the Atlantic towards Scandinavia – but sometimes it blows the opposite way, from the North East to the South West.

Test each of your samples, and note the pH. You'll probably find that if you test samples for two weeks, the pH of your rain-water does vary.

When the national Acid Drops survey was first carried out in 1985, thousands of children collected their samples and tested them, and then sent the results to a central computer.

What the scientists were able to see from all those samples was that the rain was affected by acid pollution in most places, most of the time, and that in some places it became very acid – as low as pH 4.

The most interesting thing, though, was the way the weather affected acidity. When the wind was blowing from the South West, off the 'clean' Atlantic, most areas had rain which was fairly unpolluted. When the wind blew from the North East and the East, it came from the industrial cities of central Europe, and the rain became much more acid.

In 1986, and each year since, children in other parts of Europe have also taken part in the Acid Drops project, and in Sweden, for example, the situation is different. There, if the wind is blowing from the South West, it is blowing across Britain, where it picks up the pollution from our towns and cities, and then their rain is acid. The forests of northern Germany have become so badly damaged by acid rain because wherever the wind blows from, it comes to that area from an industrial region, so the rain is always polluted.

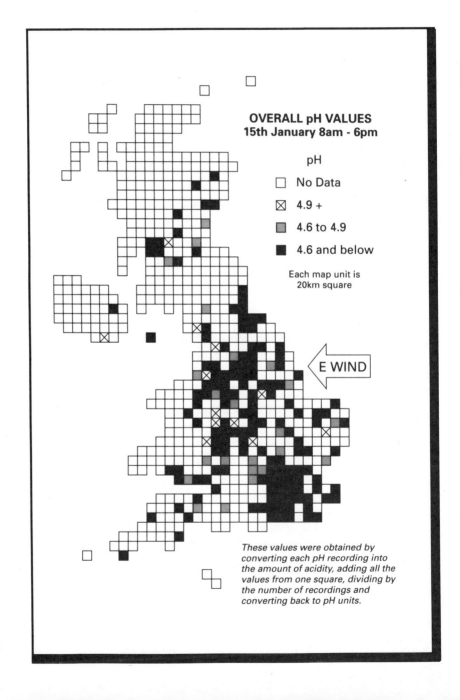

OVERALL pH VALUES
15th January 8am - 6pm

pH

☐ No Data

⊠ 4.9 +

▨ 4.6 to 4.9

■ 4.6 and below

Each map unit is
20km square

E WIND

These values were obtained by
converting each pH recording into
the amount of acidity, adding all the
values from one square, dividing by
the number of recordings and
converting back to pH units.

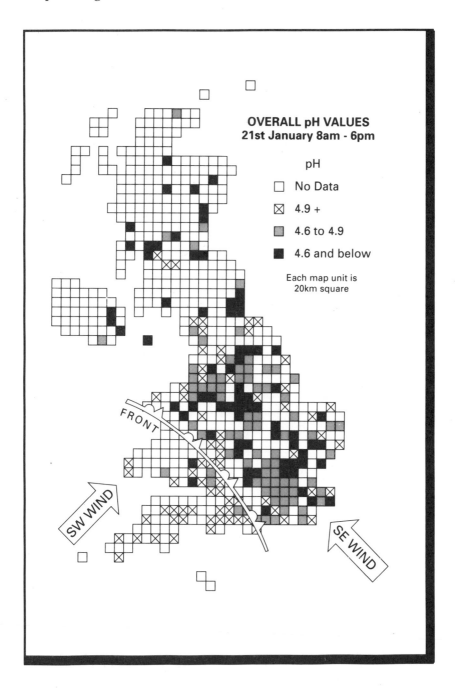

OVERALL pH VALUES
21st January 8am - 6pm

pH

☐ No Data

⊠ 4.9 +

▨ 4.6 to 4.9

■ 4.6 and below

Each map unit is
20km square

FRONT

SW WIND

SE WIND

DIAGRAMS TO HELP YOU

CUT ---------- CUT

Your rain
collector   20cm
→

FIG 1 CUTTING YOUR LEMONADE BOTTLE

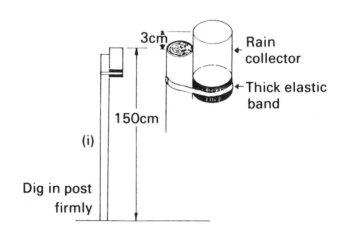

FIG 2 SETTING UP YOUR RAIN COLLECTOR

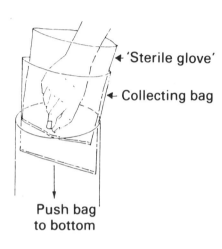

'Sterile glove'

Collecting bag

Push bag
to bottom

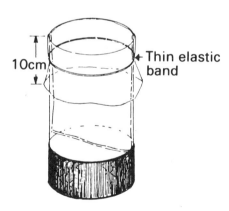

10cm

Thin elastic
band

FIG 3 FITTING THE COLLECTING BAG

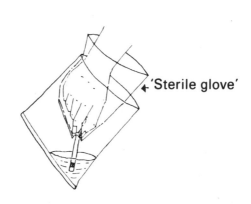

FIG 4 TESTING THE PH

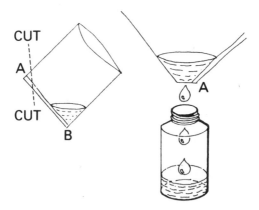

FIG 5 FILLING THE EMPTY BOTTLE

Acid drops – summary

What you're measuring

How acid the rain- (or snow) water is where you live.

What you need

Empty plastic pop-bottle.
A stake at least 1.5 metres long.
Clean polythene bags.
Rubber bands.
Some pH testing strips.
A colour chart to match your readings.

Where to sample

Anywhere that's nearby, but not overhung by trees or buildings.

When to sample

Choose a similar time each day, or evening, and sample every day for at least two weeks.

How your project can help fight pollution locally

It is difficult to be sure just where your acid rain is coming from, but if the samples are more acid whenever the wind is blowing from the direction of the local power-station or factory chimney, you should let your environmental health officer know.

Importance of the National WATCH project

Thousands of samples from all over Britain, gathered together on daily maps, have shown which kind of weather produces most acid rain, and which parts of the country are most badly affected. This has helped persuade the government that power-station clean-ups should take place more quickly.

Lichen Count

If you look in old country churchyards, you will often see strange patterns of green and brown roughness on the gravestones. These are lichens – unusual colonies of plants – and by looking out for different kinds of lichens you can get a pretty accurate picture of how clean or polluted the air is. Lichens are damaged by acids – so the kind of pollution that produces acid rain will determine which lichens grow.

This survey needs to be done over a wide area – perhaps a whole town, or at least a neighbourhood. You need to look for the different kinds of lichen that are shown on the next few pages, and you'll see that they each grow in different levels of pollution. In zone 0, you won't find any lichens at all. There is just too much acid in the air for them to survive. In most towns and villages you should be able to find lichens from zones 1, 2 and 3, but to find the 'old man's beard' lichens in zone 6, you've really got to go somewhere that's very clean indeed.

Some lichens grow on stones – especially soft, limey stones – and some grow on the bark of trees. The best specimens can usually be found in sheltered places. They are tough, and keep their shape and colour all year round, so this is a pollution survey you can do in the winter, and you can go back and check your comparisons, too, because lichens live for years.

If you want to do a simple lichen survey to test the system, choose three cemeteries. Find

- one in the middle of town, preferably among the fumes of traffic and heavy polluting industry,
- one at the edge of town, surrounded by houses and

gardens, with some traffic nearby but no serious pollution problems, and
• one out in the countryside, well away from chemical farm sprays as well as factories

You might have to wait till you go on holiday to visit the third of these. The cemeteries will probably each have a different range of lichens growing in them.

To do the survey more scientifically, you need a map of your survey area. An Ordnance Survey 'Town Map' is ideal. Mark on it any factories or other places such as bus stations or power stations which you suspect of producing pollution, and find out which way the wind blows most of the time. Remember that in most of Britain the prevailing wind blows from the South West to the North East – Devon to Northumberland – but the shape of the land can alter that.

Now, carry out your lichen survey starting close to the suspected source of pollution, and moving further and further away in the direction that the prevailing wind blows. Search the trunks of old trees, garden walls, gravestones and any other surface you think might have lichen growing on them, and see if there is a pattern to the pollution.

You would expect the lichens to show cleaner air as you move further away, but you may be surprised. A tall chimney might throw the smoke a long way, and cause the worst pollution at quite a distance.

If you carry out a lichen survey for the whole town, then it will show which areas have clean air and which areas are polluted – and remember, this isn't just a measure of pollution at one particular time. Lichens show up the pollution we have been breathing for years.

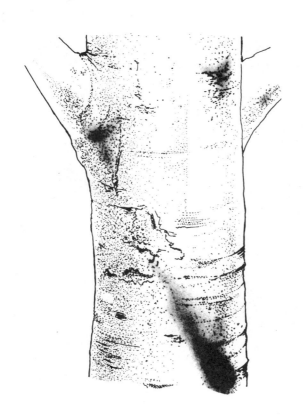

Zone 0. No lichens

Serious air pollution means a 'lichen desert'. Of course, you need to look very thoroughly, to be quite sure you haven't missed any, and you may find a green, powdery alga (Pleurococcus) just to confuse you. It grows on smooth stone surfaces, and on the trunks of sycamore trees. You can rub it off with your fingers, but it's not a lichen.

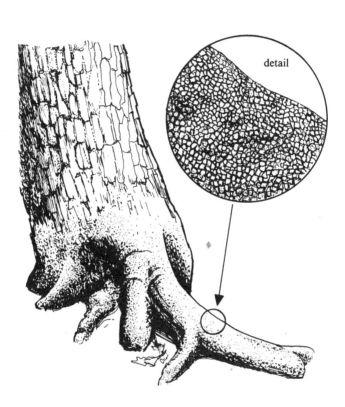

detail

Zone 1. Crusty lichens

These lichens can survive in quite high levels of pollution, so you do find these in the middle of town –especially low down around the bottom of tree trunk. If you look through a magnifying glass (or the wrong way down a pair of binoculars), you'll see that the crusty lichen are like miniature crazy paving. 'Lecanora conizaeoides' is grey green, and the most common lichen of all. 'Lecanora dispersa', is pale grey.

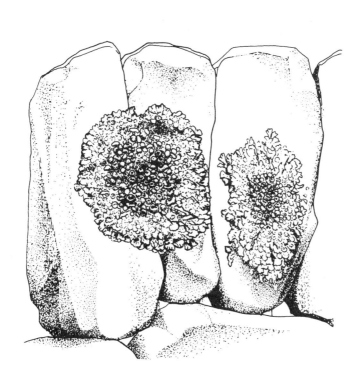

Zone 2. Orange/yellow Xanthoria

This is a pretty lichen, which grows as circular rough patches, especially on limey stone, concrete and asbestos. You often see it on the roof of farm buildings, but you never see it on trees. It grows when the air is beginning to get clean, and the reason it grows on limey materials, is because the lime helps to reduce the effect of the acid pollution.

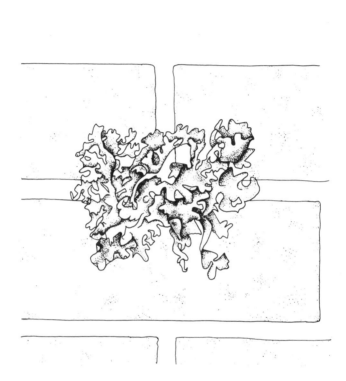

Zone 3. 'Leafy lichens' on walls

This is the first zone where the lichens really look like plants. The kind you're most likely to find is 'Parmelia saxatilis'. The colour is grey-green, and each lichen can grow to about the size of a saucer. The trees in zone 3 still only have crusty lichens and green powdery algae on them, because they can't provide any helpful liminess to balance the acid pollution.

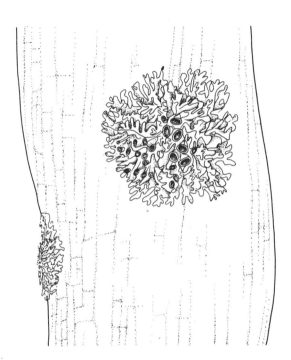

Zone 4. 'Leafy lichens' on trees

Parmelia starts to appear at the base of tree trunks once the air is free of the worst pollution. As it gets cleaner, leafy lichens grow higher and higher up the trees.

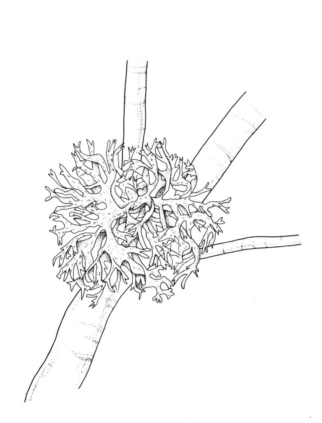

Zone 5. Shrubby lichens

These are much leafier than the flat 'leafy lichens' of zones 3 and 4, and they are a sure sign that pollution has almost disappeared. The toughest of them is called 'Evernia purnastria', and again, it's grey-green. 'Ramelina calicanis' is shinier green, a bit more upright, and may have pink tips at the ends of its 'leafy' bits.

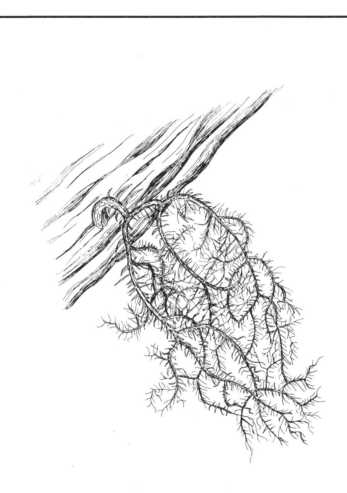

Zone 6. 'Old Man's Beard'

These really can be very straggly, and are quite common once you reach the unpolluted places. They have stems up to 15cm long and hang from trees, held on only by small, disc-shaped attachments.

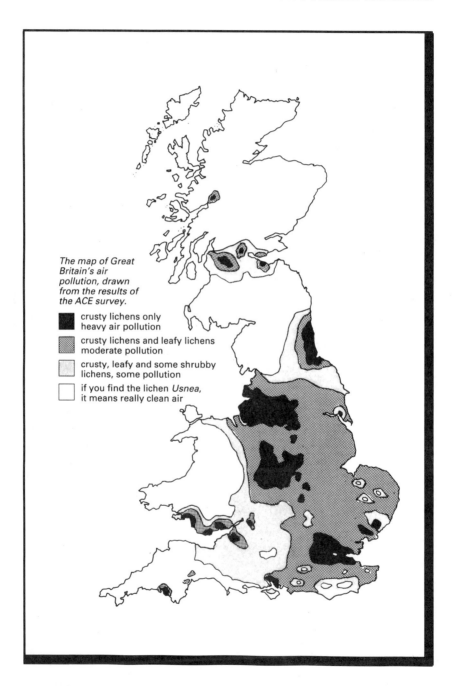

The map of Great Britain's air pollution, drawn from the results of the ACE survey.

crusty lichens only
heavy air pollution

crusty lichens and leafy lichens
moderate pollution

crusty, leafy and some shrubby
lichens, some pollution

if you find the lichen *Usnea*,
it means really clean air

Lichen Count – summary

What you're measuring

Pollution in the air you breathe. Different species of lichens can survive in different levels of pollution.

What you need

The identification pictures, a notebook and a map of the area you're surveying.

Where to sample

Anywhere, but you'll have to visit different places to find all the different kinds of lichen, and you'll probably not find any at all in very dirty, polluted industrial areas. Look out for different lichens if you go away on holiday.

When to sample

All year round – though some of the lichens will be easier to find in winter, where there are fewer leaves around to hide them.

How the project can help fight pollution locally

The lichen count will show very clearly which areas have clean air, and which are polluted. This can be especially useful if an area is surveyed for several years. You can see how pollution levels are changing.

4 Pollution is Rubbish

Solid pollution is a bit more difficult to deal with than smoke and fumes. Those bulging black polythene bags, soggy mattresses and shopping trolleys seem to appear by magic in lay-byes, and on waste land. Most of the junk arrives in a vehicle – a car boot for the small stuff, or a lorry for the large-scale dumpings – so if you're lucky you might have a number plate to identify the polluter. However, if you're going to report them, you really do need another witness to back up your story, because no one is going to admit to dumping rubbish. Sometimes there are clues in the rubbish itself. If its just bags of household waste, there might be the odd envelope, with the name and address of the dumper on it, for instance, or a lorry load of builders rubble might include some pieces of broken equipment carrying the company's name.

You must be careful when you're poking around for the clues, though. Even the most harmless pile of junk can be dangerous. It can contain poisonous chemicals – weed-killers, for instance, or sharp broken glass. It's best to report the dumping, and leave the detective work to the experts – your trusty environmental health officers.

If there's somewhere in your patch that's especially bad for dumping (the problem usually does occur in particular spots where cars can back in or lorries can drive in and out quickly), think about 'staking out' the site, and watching for polluters. The ideal camouflage is another car, so see if you can persuade a grown up to come with you, park the car and give you cover. That way, you will have an extra witness, and you will be safer.

Lorry dumping is most likely to take place at the end of the working day, when the driver is in a hurry to get home, and can't be bothered driving to the official tip. Household rubbish is more likely to be bundled out of the boot on a Sunday morning. If you are going to keep watch, don't make it too obvious. Standing there in the lay-bye with a clip-board in your hand, and your camera ready, is pretty likely to put the polluter off. Of course, if you're prepared to stand there 24 hours a day, seven days a week, 52 weeks a year, clip-board in hand, then you might actually drive the pollution problem away for good, although the polluters will probably only move on to the next dumping spot. What you should really do is work with a friend as your fellow witness. Keep notes of the time, a description of the dumpers and the rubbish, and note the number plate of their vehicles. It's not a good idea to rush out of the bushes and ask them politely to put the rubbish back in the car boot. They might just bundle you in there with it. Rubbish dumpers are breaking the law, so phone the council or the police.

Water pollution

In a country as wet as Britain, with so many ponds, ditches, streams and rivers, it's not surprising to find that a great deal of our waste ends up polluting the water. As a pollution-spotter, water pollution is the most difficult to track down. Water moves around, eventually flowing down to the sea, and because in towns, particularly, we tend to bury our streams in underground pipes, it's particularly difficult to find out where the pollution is coming from. That problem is made even more difficult because there may be several different sources of pollution draining into the same stream. Over 1,500 different waste pipes drain into the Humber estuary alone. Of course, the various pollutants will then mix together, and in the worst cases, where a number of factories pollute the same stream or river with a variety of industrial chemicals, these may even combine in the water to produce new chemicals which could be more poisonous than the original ones.

To some extent, using water-courses to get rid of waste is officially accepted, and the National Rivers Authority (NRA) issues licences which state what kinds and quantities of waste are permitted. The problem is that these permitted levels of pollution are often set higher than the rivers can cope with, and as if that wasn't bad enough, the approved levels of pollution are exceeded time and time again.

In the past, the situation was particularly difficult for the 'officials' to control. The water-boards were responsible for policing and for making sure the standards were stuck to, but they also ran the sewage works. Sewage works are a major source of pollution themselves: they are often over-loaded and don't treat all the sewage properly before it's pumped into the rivers or the sea. They are also expected to deal with the chemical waste from industry, and some of that simply can't be made safe in a normal sewage works. Obviously, while even the water-boards were major polluters themselves, it was very difficult for them to control anybody else. In 1989 the situation changed. Now, water pollution control is in the hands of a new organisation, the National Rivers Authority. The NRA is setting higher standards as it issues new permits for waste disposal. It is able to police everybody – the water-boards included – so now when people cause water pollution they aren't so likely to get away with it.

When it comes to water pollution-spotting, the problems you can see most easily are not necessarily the ones that cause most damage. The easiest thing to spot is the junk. In the countryside, particularly, farm ponds are favourite dumping places. Everything, from old fertiliser bags and chemical containers, to washing machines and even wrecked tractors, seems to end up there.

In towns, our canals and streams seem to be slowly filling up with super-market trolleys, and many of the plastic bags and cans that blow around the streets end up in the water. A lot of this kind of pollution is relatively harmless to wildlife. Indeed, many of the creatures in a canal or stream will find shelter in an old tin can.

For centuries, the fishermen of the Mediterranean have used clay pots and bottles, scattered on the bed of the sea, to trap octopus and squid. These sea creatures simply regard them as another handy hole to hide in. In North America (where else?) whole underwater fish-breeding reefs have been built on the floor of reservoirs, using old car and lorry tyres, or even piles of scrap cars themselves.

Junk in water may be relatively harmless to wildlife, but nevertheless, it is a problem. First of all it looks messy, and that's especially true of the modern light-weight polystyrene plastics. They float on the surface, and last forever. Where the rubbish is allowed to build up, it seems to act as a sign to polluters that this is a good place to dump more rubbish, and so the problem gets worse.

The second problem with rubbish is water is that some of it *can* be dangerous, to people and to wildlife. Every year there are terrible accidents where people paddle in 'clean' shallow water, and stand on open tin cans, broken glass or sharp lumps of metal.

Farm animals that wade into the water to drink can suffer the same problems, too, swallowing plastic bags as they drink, for instance. Thousands of wild birds die every year, because they pick up lengths of fishing line in streams and rivers, and become fatally entangled.

Finally, although much of the junk may be relatively harmless, some things can cause very serious chemical pollution, and that's a disaster in water. An electric toy, or a torch, for instance, might sink to the bottom of the pond and lie there harmlessly for years, but the batteries inside it will soon begin to corrode. The outer skin will start to leak, and the water will be poisoned by the chemicals inside – and the chemicals in most batteries are very poisonous, indeed. The tin cans and plastic bottles a farmer dumps will never be completely free of the pesticides and other chemicals they contained, and since they are extremely concentrated, even a few millilitres may be enough to poison a pond or stream. Abandoned machinery will always have oil and grease on its moving parts, and in the case of an old vehicle, there will be a great deal of it. The kind of people who dump wrecked cars in ponds and rivers are not likely to drain the oil from the engine and gear-box first, so that oil will inevitably leak out, float to the surface, cut off the oxygen, and pollute the water.

For all these reasons, rubbish clearance is very worthwhile thing to do. It's worth doing as a big, noisy, fun event, where lots of people have a great time, splashing around, making loads of noise and cleaning up a whole problem area completely. The more people you involve, the more likely you are to prick the conscience of the dumpers themselves.

Clearing junk from ponds and streams

Safety and timing are both very important. Make sure you never try pulling junk out of streams and ponds unless there are some older people with you. They're always handy to have around to do the heavy work anyway, but more importantly, they will be able to take responsibility for the whole project. To do it properly takes a bit of organisation, and clearing junk from water really can be quite dangerous. Stick to clearing rubbish from shallow water only. The top of your wellingtons is a good depth gauge – say a maximum depth of 30cm, and to be absolutely sure its safe before you wade in, poke a stick down to the bottom. If it pushes down into soft mud, keep out.

Choose late summer. That is the time of year when you'll do the least amount of damage to the wildlife. Many water species spend the winter months hibernating in the mud, so they are easily disturbed at that time. In the spring and early summer there may well be birds nesting, and a great many other creatures breeding, too.

Arrange for the rubbish to be taken away. There is nothing worse than spending all Sunday pulling rubbish out of the water, only to find that by Monday morning it has all been thrown back in again. If you're well organised, you should be able to persuade either the council or the National Rivers Authority to provide some skips right by the waterside, but make sure they agree to collect them as soon as the clean-up is completed.

Not much equipment is really necessary for most clean-ups. Some protective clothing is useful. Wellies with steel toecaps are a good idea if there is likely to be any sharp metal amongst the rubbish, and certainly everyone should be wearing thick 'industrial' gloves. When you're pulling and tugging at rubbish under water it's very easy to cut yourself. A first aid box, plus someone in charge who knows what to do in an emergency, are essential.

Some of the junk may actually be valuable, or at least recyclable. If there is a lot of metal, keep it in a separate skip and arrange for the local scrap merchant to collect it.

One final word of warning. Before you make too many plans to remove water-rubbish, just check with the local environmental health officer at the council that it's actually safe to go splashing around in your particular pond or stream. Some water is infected with a particularly dangerous virus – Weils disease – which is spread by rats, and you can catch it very easily, particularly if you cut yourself in the water. If there is a disease problem, then you must leave the clean-up to properly equipped experts – but make sure they do get on and do it. Find yourself some clean pollution to tackle in another stream.

As a further safety precaution, make sure all the volunteer pollution cleaners have had an injection to protect them from another disease – tetanus – which is caught through dirty cuts and scratches. Finally, make sure someone – the local council, the adult group leader or the National Rivers Authority arranges insurance, just in case there is a serious accident.

When you've successfully cleaned up your stretch of water, try to stop it happening again. Put up a notice explaining who cleaned it up and make it more difficult for dumpers to get to the water's edge.

Cleaning junk from ponds and streams – summary

What you need

Wellies, water-proofs and thick gloves.
Rope for pulling out the big junk.
Plastic sacks for collecting the rubbish.
A first-aid kit.
An adult who can swim.

Where to go

You have to go where the junk is, but choose a place that local people know – one which would be a real beauty-spot if it was cleaned up.

What time of year to clean up

Autumn and winter are best – otherwise your clean-up will seriously disturb the wildlife habitat.

Solid 'junk' pollution is fairly easy to deal with, provided you can raise enough physical energy — but it's not the most serious problem. Most of the worst water pollution doesn't just sink conveniently to the bottom, and sit there waiting to be pulled out again. It is dumped either as a liquid, or as fine particles, and the flowing water is expected to take it away. The hope is that eventually it will either settle to the bottom in a thin layer, or it will be converted by the natural process of decomposition to harmless, non-polluting chemicals, or it will become so diluted that it can no longer be called pollution. This may not happen until it flows right down to the sea.

As a pollution spotter, some of this 'liquid' pollution is very easy to see, and if you can see it, then you will often be able to follow it back up-stream, and find the pipe it's pouring out of. The first thing you'll probably notice is discoloured water. In some places, particularly where there is a lot of cloth dyeing for example, the water may even change colour – pink one day; orange the next. In coal-mining areas, streams can be jet-black – completely clouded with particles of coal that have washed from waste tips or been pumped up from underground. In parts of Cornwall streams have been known to flow white, polluted with fine waste from the china clay quarries.

Beware though. After heavy rain a stream or river will often become muddy, particularly if it flows through cultivated farmland where the bare earth can wash off the waterside fields, and you can find quite bright colours in nature. If there is iron-ore in the surrounding rocks, then a stream can be bright orange, and no amount of searching will lead you to a polluting factory.

Some 'liquid' pollution floats on the surface. Many of the sewage works alongside our streams and rivers produce a continuous trail of soap-suds, because they can't cope with the contents of all our washing machines, baths, dishwashers and kitchen sinks. Soap breaks the surface tension of the water – the kind of 'skin' that pond skates and other small creatures are normally able to walk on – so soap and detergent pollution is very damaging to watery wildlife habitat.

Oils are the other major floating pollution. In fact, if there's soap there as well, it will help to break down the oil, but two wrongs don't make a right. It's much better to prevent the pollution getting into the water in the first place, rather than depending on the various chemicals to sort one another out.

With some liquid pollution, the most obvious evidence is found in the layer of green slime, or algae, that appears on the surface of the water. If there are a lot of nutrients in the water – nitrates, phosphates and other 'fertilisers' – then they will tend to encourage water plants to grow, but green plants need sunlight and oxygen as well as fertiliser. The floating plants – blanket weed, duck weed and so on – grow like mad on the surface, where they can absorb oxygen directly from the air, and where they are not shaded from the sun. That blanket of green shuts off the light to the plants down below, so they eventually die.

Gradually the amount of green slime builds up, and the lower layers of that die too. They sink to the bottom, and in decomposing they use up the oxygen that is dissolved in the water. That oxygen is vital for the fish, and many of the other water creatures, so gradually they die too. A stream that looks very lush and green is probably too richly fertilised for its own good.

WATCH on Stream

WARNING. Water can be dangerous. Never collect samples on your own.

The creatures that live in a stream or river give a good clue to the quality of the water. A clean, unpolluted stream will have lots of different creatures in it, while in a polluted stream there will be far fewer creatures, and only the very tough ones will stand a chance of surviving.

In the first ever WATCH project in 1971, over 10,000 children 'went fishing' to find out just what was living in their local stream or river, and in 1978 the survey was repeated. This project provides a measure of the amount of oxygen in the water, so it's good for finding organic pollution – the kind you get from farmyard run-off or sewage works waste – because that tends to encourage the algal growth that eventually rots down, and steals the oxygen. Inorganic chemical pollution – the kind that might come from a factory or a garage – really needs to be left to the scientists to test with their expensive scientific equipment. However, as you sample for water-creatures, if you find a stretch of water just downstream from a factory, with little or no life in it, it is well worth contacting the scientists at either the National Rivers Authority or the local Environmental Health Department of the council, and asking them to test the water.

What you need

1 Wellington boots
2 A net. Ideally this should be quite big – about the size of a carrier bag – and have a wire frame around the neck, to

keep it open. You can buy special nets for stream sampling, or the school or wildlife group may have some, but you can make a very good one using a wire coat-hanger, a thick cane or a broom handle, and the top half of a pair of old ladies' tights (but always make sure you remove the old lady first).

3 A specimen tray. A plastic egg box, or an ice-cube tray is useful. You're looking for as many different creatures as you can find, so with a specimen tray like this you can put each type into a different little compartment. A white washing-up bowl is also useful for the first sorting.

4 Identification check sheet. It's not just fish you're trying to catch in your fishing net, it's creepy-crawlies –aquatic invertebrates to give them their posh title – the worms, shellfish and insect larvae that live in streams and rivers. The WATCH stream survey pack has a clever sliding chart to help give the water a pollution score. The chart below will help you identify what you find, and that will give you an accurate idea of how clean the stream is.

Indicators – from least polluted to most polluted

1 Stonefly nymph	10 Freshwater shrimp
2 Flattened mayfly nymph	11 Caseless caddis larva
3 Damselfly nymph	12 Snails
4 Cased caddis larva	13 Flatworm
5 Limpet	14 Waterlouse
6 Blackfly larva	15 Non-red midge larva
7 Beetle	16 Sludgeworm
8 Swimming mayfly larva	17 Bloodworm
9 Alderfly larva	18 Rat-tailed maggot

Where to sample

It's best to choose small streams for your sampling. They're the safest for you, and they're also the ones most easily polluted by small amounts of organic waste. Keep away from big rivers and deep water.

Choose a stream where the bank is easy to get up and down. Sample the water where there's plenty of sunlight – you'll find more of the wildlife living there.

What time of year to sample

You can sample at any time, but there is far more life in the water between spring and autumn. Winter sampling isn't very good, and it freezes your toes, too. April and October are probably the best months of all for good results.

How to sample

For the best results you need to stand in the water, facing downstream. Stick the net into the water and push firmly down onto the bottom, so the neck faces upstream towards your wellies. If you shuffle your feet gently, that will loosen any creatures clinging to the stones, and they'll float down into your net.

Empty the 'catch' very gently into clear water in your bowl or specimen tray. Remember, these are living animals, and you can damage them if you're rough. It's also much harder to identify them from the chart, if most of their legs have been snapped off because you weren't gentle enough.

When you have identified your creatures, and made notes of the different types, put them carefully back into the water. To make the survey even more thorough, sample for a fixed time – say 5 minutes – and count the total number you catch, as well as the number of different types. Lots of good ones mean a *very* clean river. Very few and only 'bad' indicator species mean serious pollution.

How to use the WATCH Streams Survey

The national survey was able to compare pollution levels all over the country. Tens of thousands of people sent their results in to WATCH, and maps were produced, showing which parts of the country had the cleanest rivers. For individuals or small groups, the most useful thing to do is choose a stretch of stream or small river, and take samples every 100 metres or so along its length. If you do that, keeping a record of each sampling point, and which indicator species you find, you will build up a picture of the way pollution levels change along the stream. That also helps find the source of pollution.

If you take two samples, and the one upstream has lots of damselfly nymphs and caddis-fly larvae in it, while the one downstream only has bloodworms and sludge-worms living in it, you can be sure that somewhere between the two there's a serious source of organic pollution getting into the water. Usually you can spot smelly liquid from a farm or factory trickling out of a pipe or a side-ditch.

If you do the same survey, in the same places, at the same time each year, you can see if the stream is becoming more or less polluted.

Here are the results that some of the WATCH water surveys came up with.

• Two sisters in Yorkshire, Fiona and Louise Dalton, carried out surveys on streams passing two fish farms. One was found to have reasonably clear water above and below the farm, but at the other, the girls discovered a different story. They found that while the stream above the fish farm was clear and unpolluted, below the fish farm outflow, the stream was polluted with fish droppings and had very little life in it apart from a large quantity of midge larvae. The Yorkshire Water Authority responded quickly to their findings, and advised the fish farm to install a settlement lagoon to catch the fish droppings before they reached the stream.

* Again in Yorkshire a WATCH group found a stream was being seriously polluted with pig slurry or silage effluent. The Yorkshire Water Authority was informed, and decided to prosecute the farmer responsible for the pollution.

* An environmental studies group from Bridlington School found high nitrate levels in a local stream, which were probably coming from nearby farmland. They called on the farmers to stop dumping their chemical waste and in return, a group of volunteers helped to clear discarded litter, bottles and cans from the water.

* The Torridge WATCH Group in Devon were sampling a stream near Torrington on a Sunday afternoon, when it suddenly turned black! The unpleasant gunge was traced to a large abattoir which had just washed out a waste storage tank, releasing a gush of 'trade effluent' into the stream. The incident was reported to the South West Water Authority. They fined the company and made sure that in future it would deal with its waste more carefully.

* The Hertfordshire and Middlesex Wildlife Trust 'Living Rivers Project' came up with the alarming facts that only 9 per cent of the sites tested could be graded as good, while 41 per cent were medium, and 50 per cent came out as having poor water quality.

Keep going back

It's very unusual to find a source of pollution, to get it stopped, and to solve the problem instantly. If it's industrial there may be a need to build a new piece of machinery in the factory. If it's on a farm an extra waste tank may need digging first, or if it's traffic pollution, the offending bus garage may clean up its own vehicles, but there will always be lorries travelling through from elsewhere, and some of them may be even worse than the buses. From your point of view, carrying out tests and surveys, and measuring the levels of pollution, are even more valuable if you can keep going back, and measuring pollution levels again and again.

That's what the WATCH groups in Hertfordshire have done with their clean rivers project. They did their first sampling in the 1970s, and that gave them a picture of where there was bad water pollution, and also, of course, where the water was cleanest. The various WATCH groups in the county have gone back to those same streams, ponds and rivers ever since, and they have built up a unique record of the way pollution levels have changed.

In the case of Hertfordshire, the evidence from the pollution spotters has helped identify some particularly bad polluters, and the worst of them have been cleaned up. The WATCH groups have also shown that, while there are fewer extreme cases of water pollution now than there were when the survey began, the over-all level of pollution has actually got slightly worse. What is especially interesting is the way rural rivers, which flow through the farming countryside, have become more polluted with farm chemicals. At the same time the dirty industries in the built-up areas have cleaned up or closed down, and so urban water pollution has been reduced as a result.

STONEFLY NYMPH
(up to 30mm)

Two long tails. Crawls very
slowly in fast running water.
Gills not normally obvious.

SWIMMING MAYFLY NYMPH
(up to 11mm)

Spindle-shaped body. Three
tails. Swims by beating its
body up and down.

FLATTENED MAYFLY NYMPH
(up to 16mm)

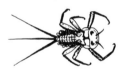

Flat with moon-shaped head,
large flat legs. Gills along
body.

CASELESS CADDISFLY LARVA
(up to 28mm)

Well-marked head and three
pairs of legs. Gills along or
under the body with hooks at
the tail.

CASED CADDISFLY LARVA
(up to 55mm)

Lives in a case of sand,
stones, twigs or pieces of leaf.
Crawls dragging its case.

FRESHWATER SHRIMP
(up to 20mm)

Swims on its side very
quickly. Colour varies from
reddish to grey.

WATER LOUSE (up to 12mm)  Greyish-brown, flat, very like a woodlouse. Crawls.	SLUDGE WORM (up to 40mm)  Like a small earthworm. Dull reddish-brown colour.
BLOODWORM (OR MIDGE LARVA) (up to 20mm) Bright red. Thick and stumpy. Swims quickly with looping movements.	RAT-TAILED MAGGOT (up to 55mm incl. tube)  Grey. Fat body and a very long tube to breathe air at the water's surface.

DAMSELFLY NYMPH (up to 30mm)  Slender. Large head. Three tails which act as flat gills. Body moves side to side when swimming.	LIMPET (up to 20mm)  Small shell which is neither spiral nor coiled. Like a tiny cup.
BLACKFLY LARVA (up to 15mm)  End of body swollen. Moves by looping. Often attached to stones by sucker.	ALDERFLY LARVA (up to 40mm)  Long gills trail from side of body. Stout brownish body, with single tail.
BEETLE (up to 38mm) 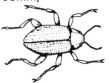 Most small beetles in streams can't swim but crawl slowly hanging on with hooks on their legs.	SNAILS (up to 50mm)  Hard shells, which may be coiled or spiral.

FLATWORM
(up to 40mm)

Very flat. Sometimes have
'tentacles' or tiny eye spots.
Glides over stream bottom.

NON-RED MIDGE LARVA
(up to 20mm)

Like the bloodworm, but green
or brown.

BLANKET WEED

Long green threads found in
enormous sheets in polluted
water.

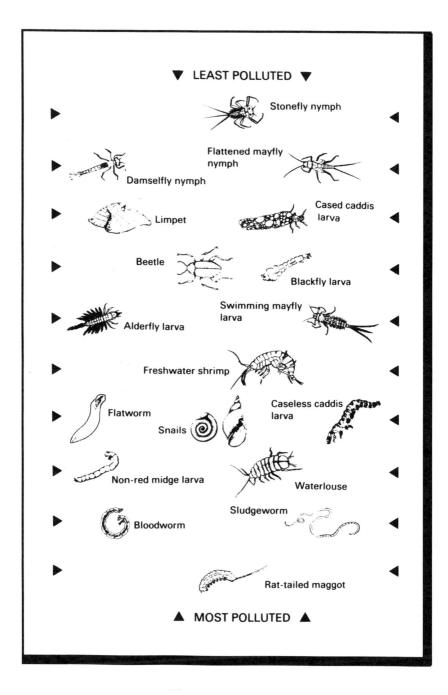

▼ LEAST POLLUTED ▼

Stonefly nymph

Flattened mayfly nymph

Damselfly nymph

Limpet

Cased caddis larva

Beetle

Blackfly larva

Alderfly larva

Swimming mayfly larva

Freshwater shrimp

Flatworm

Snails

Caseless caddis larva

Non-red midge larva

Waterlouse

Sludgeworm

Bloodworm

Rat-tailed maggot

▲ MOST POLLUTED ▲

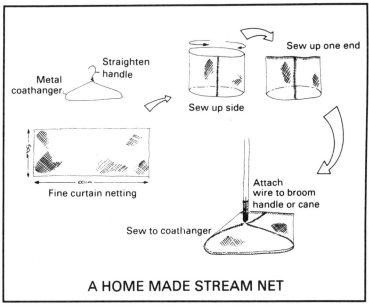

A HOME MADE STREAM NET

WATCH on Stream – summary

What you are measuring

Levels of water pollution, using wildlife indicators.

What you need

Wellies and waterproofs.
A net, specimen tray and the check sheet.

Where to sample

Safe shallow water upstream and downstream of a polluting inlet, for most dramatic results.

When to sample

Spring and autumn.

How your project can help stop local pollution

This is a good way of showing where the cleanest and the dirtiest water is. Do enough sampling and you can start to show where the pollution is getting into the streams and rivers.

How the WATCH on Stream Project has helped tackle pollution nationally

Lots of sampling, over several years, has produced a picture of which water is getting cleaner, and where pollution is getting worse. That has helped increase the pressure to stop the polluters.

5 Tackling Pollution

It is very useful to measure pollution levels and build up detailed records of how the problem is changing, but we need to do more than that. We need to do everything we can to reduce the problem itself.

Helping the natural processes to deal with organic 'bio-degradable' waste

Where pollution is caused by bio-degradable waste, quite often the problem is simply one of 'overloading' the system. A healthy river can convert sewage or farm slurry to harmless materials, but not in the quantities we often expect it to cope with. A lot of the litter we throw away will eventually rot down, but not if it's dumped in a big soggy heap. There are a whole range of ways, both large-scale and small-scale, in which nature can be 'helped along'.

Add more air

In this wet country of ours, it is often a lack of oxygen that limits the effectiveness of a decomposing process. The stream or river flows along slowly, and once its oxygen is used up, the natural organisms that work on the sewage and other organic pollutants can't do their job. A simple sewage works – one of those places with circular raised beds and merry-go-rounds of dribbling pipes – is designed to put more oxygen back into the water, so the natural micro-organisms can work more effectively on the sewage.

The mixture of sewage and water trickles through a deep layer of crushed stone, so it flows as a very thin film of liquid, rather than a single stream. That allows more oxygen to be dissolved from the air, and the natural clean-up process is given a boost. Problems only really occur if the bits of plastic, rubber and other 'unmentionables' we flush down the loo manage to get through the various filters, and block up the dribbler nozzles, or when poisonous chemicals are poured down the drain and kill the useful micro-organisms. Often that kind of chemical pollution comes from industry as a waste product, but the system also suffers from ordinary householders who use the sink and toilet as waste disposal points, and pour down such things as unused paint, garden pesticides and car engine oil. Even the detergents from washing machines and dish-washers can foul up the sewage works if they become too concentrated.

The organic pollution problems in a stream or river can be reduced by building low dams. As the water flows over the top, it gets stirred up and oxygen is absorbed, so a good waterfall or an old-fashioned water-wheel helps speed up water pollution clean-up very effectively.

On a larger scale, oxygen is sometimes pumped into polluted lakes and rivers mechanically, as an aid to the clean-up process. This certainly works, but it generally uses pumps which are driven by diesel, or electricity generated in a power station, so in cleaning up pollution in the water, the process adds to pollution in the air.

Natural aeration of a water-course is much healthier, but in the past 40 or 50 years, big machines have been used by drainage engineers to change many of our streams and rivers. In order to make them flow faster, and help drain water from the surrounding farmland, the river-beds have been straightened and rapids and waterfalls have been levelled. That now means less aeration, and less natural effect on organic pollution.

Re-oxygenating streams

If you find a small stream, perhaps polluted with organic waste from a farm, then building dams across it, to create lots of shallow waterfalls, will put more oxygen back in the stream, and help nature clean up the problem.

What you need

Wellies and thick waterproof gloves
Damming material – railway sleepers, old crates filled with stones, concrete kerbstones.

Where to do it

In shallow, slow-flowing streams where it's safe and easy to get down into the water. Ask the National Rivers Authority for permission, and the people who own the bank on either side.

When to do it

The winter months are best. You will cause least disturbance to the wildlife then.

Effect on pollution

Splashing a little more oxygen into polluted water allows more clean-up organisms to live there. One or two small dams can help the water to clean itself.

Increasing the organisms

The cleaning of organic water pollution is actually done by a whole range of plants and animals that live on the waste. If they are present in healthy numbers, and there is plenty of oxygen available, then as farm waste sewage, or other organic material flows down stream, it will become less and less concentrated as these helpful organisms deal with it.

In Denmark, scientists have developed a clever way of increasing the effectiveness of the helpful plants and animals. They build a series of big tanks the size of mini-swimming pools, and let the polluted liquid flow through them. In tank one there are lots of algae – very simple plants that grow to form a green slime. A slime that lives on sewage sounds delightful but that is exactly what happens.

With plenty of oxygen in the water, the algae take up the pollutants, in particular nitrates, ammonia and phosphates. The polluted water is re-circulated through the slime tank several times using a little electric pump. The scientists even have sheets of carpet underlay hanging in the water, to give the algae a bigger surface to grow on. After four or five days this water has lost most of its original pollution and generated a great deal of slime instead.

The next tank contains two kinds of animals: thousands and thousands of tiny creatures called daphnae, that can feed on the algae, and a shoal of fish to stop the daphnae getting out of control.

The fish and the daphnae between them clean up the green algae, but the water still isn't pure – so then it passes into a third tank which contains snails and fresh-water mussels. Both these simple creatures live on the waste from the fish in tank number two, and they are so efficient that by the time the water flows out of the system and into the stream, it is much much less polluted. It does still contain some fertility, and to make full use of that, the Danish scientists are planning to use it for irrigation, to feed and water food crops.

This really is a very simple idea. In effect the scientists have taken the helpful plants and animals that deal with organic pollution in a natural stream, and concentrated them in one small area where they can keep an eye on them. It is possible to harvest the fish, the mussels and the crop-plants, too, so this pollution treatment system can help produce food. That should make it particularly valuable in the poorer countries of the third world, where sewage often flows straight into rivers in such concentrations that all the helpful organisms are killed.

Reed-beds as natural clean-up habitat

There is one kind of wildlife habitat that is especially effective at cleaning up pollution. In fact, it can even tackle some of the man-made chemicals produced by industry. Reed-beds are wonderful natural filters. They occur in nature where a stream or river slows down and spreads out to form a shallow wetland. The most obvious organisms are the reeds themselves. Usually they are a species of tall grass called 'Phragmites communis', which grows in still water up to one metre deep, and can reach over three metres in height.

This is the same reed that is cut traditionally for thatching roofs, and you often see it growing in the shallows around the shoreline of lakes, or in wet ditches. Quite often the reeds will be mixed in with another tall grass-like water-plant, which most people call bulrush or reed mace. Its scientific name is 'Typha'.

The pollution treatment works best if the polluted water flows through the mud the reeds are growing in. The matt of dead reed stems on the surface has some filtering effect, but again, it's oxygen that is the main clean-up factor. In order to grow in the waterlogged mud, the reeds' roots must have lots of oxygen. The plants are able to pull oxygen into their leaves from the surrounding air, and then pump it down the stems and out through the roots – so the mud the reeds grow in is oxygen enriched. As the organically polluted water flows through it, the oxygen enrichment helps the biological cleaning action to work efficiently.

Reed-beds are a very rich and diverse wildlife habitat. Many special birds live in British reed-beds. Perhaps the rarest is the bittern – a big brown bird, related to the heron, which is very secretive. Often the only clue you have that there are bitterns about is the deep booming call of the male birds, when they are attracting mates and defending territory in the spring and early summer. They sound as though they are blowing over the open neck of an empty bottle.

Many species of wildfowl feed in among the reed-beds, either on the seed of the Phragmites, or on the animal life that shares the habitat, and there are other, smaller birds that nest up amongst the reed stems: sedge warblers, bearded tits and reed buntings, for instance.

Other birds simply use the wet reed-beds as a safe place to roost. Thousands of starlings may descend at dusk, and swallows gather in this habitat in the autumn, and build up their fat reserves by feeding on the clouds of insects before migrating 4,000 miles south for their African winter.

Otters are one of the rarest of the reed-bed mammals we have. They enjoy the watery secrecy. Of course, there is a huge variety of insects and other invertebrates that thrive in the habitat, too. All in all, reed-beds are pretty special places for wildlife.

Sadly, most of our reed-beds have been drained and destroyed to make way for more farmland or new buildings, but they are so valuable, both as wildlife habitat and as a pollution treatment process, that new reed-beds are now being created again, particularly on wet land alongside polluted streams and rivers.

Any reed-bed will help clean up the water that passes through it, so our existing reed-bed nature-reserves are doing a good job already. In North East England, one parks department has dug up an area of mown grassland to create a ½ha reed-bed, to clean up sewage pollution from a small but smelly stream, and on a much grander scale, ICI is creating a large new reed-bed in the grounds of its chemical works beside the river Tees. The company has decided this is the most effective way of removing polluting chemicals called phenols, before the waste liquid is allowed to pour into the river. In West Germany, whole villages, and even a town of 60,000 inhabitants, now clean their polluted sewage water using reed-bed technology.

Organic waste on dry land

Not all the organic waste we produce ends up in the water. A great deal of it stays on or in the land, and can cause serious pollution problems there. In agriculture, for instance, when the combine harvesters gather in the corn, they leave behind the stems, or straw. Where a farmer produces animals as well as plant crops, that straw is useful as bedding, and when mixed with the animal droppings it can eventually be returned to the fields as farmyard manure. The pollution problem has arisen because farms have become very specialised, and the areas of the country producing most of the straw are generally a long way from those with farm animals, so the straw has become a problem waste product. Given enough time, the micro-organisms in the soil *should* be able to deal with the straw. Worms can pull it down into the earth, where all the other plants and animals of decomposition can work on it. However, intensive arable crop-land isn't usually given the chance to rest between crops, and because the same kind of crops are grown year after year, the soil itself doesn't work so well. The farmers' solution, for a number of years now, has been to burn the straw on the fields – creating clouds of polluting black smoke, damaging the wildlife, occasionally setting fire to hedgerows and trees, and adding to the problem of the greenhouse effect by producing more carbon dioxide. In 1992, at long last, this polluting practice is being banned in Britain.

City parks' departments sweep up thousands of tons of leaves each autumn, clearing them from sports pitches, footpaths and roads. Most of these leaves are burned to get rid of them, or else they are dumped in a hole in the ground somewhere.

At house and garden level, almost half the contents of the average dustbin is bio-degradable organic waste. That includes all the potato peelings, cabbage leaves, egg shells and other vegetable waste, but it also includes paper and cardboard – in fact, almost everything that isn't glass, plastic or metal. Add to that all the lawn clippings, hedge trimmings and weeds that a garden produces, and it's easy to see what an enormous mountain of rottable waste we're throwing away each year. Most of it joins those park leaves in a hole in the ground. Landfill sites are becoming more and more difficult to find. We're running out, and quite often an old quarry or a gravel pit that is a really valuable wildlife site is destroyed as a rubbish dump.

The environmental damage caused by land-fill isn't restricted to the loss of nice holes in the ground. All that waste has to be transported. Usually it travels by road in bin-lorries which burn fossils fuels, pollute the atmosphere themselves and slow down the rest of the road-users, making them more polluting, too.

Once in the ground, the waste is covered over and starved of oxygen. The organic materials – the grass clippings, cabbage leaves and the rest – decompose very slowly, producing a number of gases, known collectively as biogas. This contains methane and carbon monoxide – two of the most serious of the polluting gases which are causing the greenhouse effect.

The more modern landfill sites are now being planned and managed very carefully, with pipes built into the layers of waste material, so that the biogas can be collected, and then burned or used as a fuel to generate electricity. That is obviously an improvement, but even so, if the waste can be dealt with where it is first produced, that does much less environmental damage.

If everyone of us put our biodegradable rubbish on a compost heap, instead of dumping it in the bin, this would save the country's councils an estimated £200 million each year.

Making a compost heap

You don't need a lot of room for a compost heap, but you do need quite a lot of patience, and good compost-making involves a bit of hard work. Here are the basic rules:

Build a box to hold the compost. Ideally this should be in a quiet corner, handy for the source of organic waste – the kitchen, for instance – but not in a spot where you have to look at it all day long. The sight of rotting vegetables may be fascinating, but only in small doses.

Remember:

- Air needs to get into your heap, so don't build the box with solid sides. Use wire-netting fixed to posts, or boards with gaps between. If you can get them, the easiest thing to use is a set of three old lorry pallets – those wooden platforms that are used for loading things onto lorries using fork-lift trucks. Fix the three pallets so they stand on their edge, and make an open-fronted box.
- The 'compost-making' creatures live naturally in the soil. Build your compost on loose bare-ground, so that they can creep up into it.
- Compost works best if it gets very warm, and not too wet – so put a lid on the heap. The best thing to use is a lump of old carpet – the kind without foam backing. That will let air and some rain through, but keep the heat in, and it's easy to lift off and on.
- Build two compost boxes if you have room. Even

when the heap is complete, it takes quite a while for the composting creatures to do the job – six or seven weeks in summer, and three or four months in the cold of winter. It's useful to be building one heap while the other is composting.

What to do

Once the box is built, you can start using it to fight pollution. It can take anything that will rot down, and eventually turn it into a useful fertilizer for the garden. For the best and fastest compost-making, follow these rules:

- Put coarse material on the bottom of the heap – twigs and sticks, for instance. They won't rot down very quickly, but they create air spaces, and if some oxygen can flow right under the heap there will be more rapid composting activity in the middle.
- Build the heap quickly. See if any of your neighbours want to provide you with their kitchen waste, and look around for other things to build up your compost heap.
- Avoid big lumps or very hard things in the heap. If you put a whole cabbage on your compost heap, for instance, it will rot down eventually, but it takes a long time for the composting creatures to eat their way in. Chop it into small pieces and it will work much better. Sticks are best kept to the bottom of the heap, or used elsewhere. You could build a hibernation heap for hedgehogs, perhaps.
- As you build up the heap, walk about on it from time to time, to press it down. If it is too loose, it won't heat up enough to kill the weed seeds, and then when you come to use the compost you'll have problems with weeds.

Don't make it too compact, though, or you'll stop air getting in and the heap will just go soggy.

- Turn the whole heap right over completely at least once. When the box is full, leave the heap for a week or two, with the lid on to let the heat build up. When you're feeling fit, pull the whole heap apart, mix it up again and rebuild it so the material on the outside gets moved to the hotter centre. If you have two compost boxes, you can transfer the whole heap from the first to the second at this stage, and then start building a new one.

When you do this job you'll be amazed how many creatures there are living in the heap. You will probably be joined by the local robins, always keen to snap up a free lunch.

What you can compost

Remember, anything you can convert to compost in your heap is saving the polluting, energy-wasting journey in the council bin-lorry, and the problems of being dumped in a hole in the ground.

You can make good compost from a wide range of things, but basically you're looking for anything that is soft, easy to make soggy, and that has come from a plant. That obviously includes autumn leaves, and all the potato peelings, cabbage leaves, onion and banana skins, apple cores and other kitchen waste; anything that isn't meat. Meat tends to attract rats and other scavengers, so that should still go in the dustbin.

Garden waste can go on the compost heap, too. Weeds and soft hedge-clippings will all rot down, but lawn mowings need to be mixed in with coarse material, or otherwise they just go soggy, and stop air circulating. If you keep pets, their bedding can go on the compost heap, and even newspaper and cardboard will rot down, though again it's better to tear it into bits first. Otherwise it blocks air movement. Composting is quite a good alternative to recycling for newspapers. The energy and pollution involved in driving bundles of paper to a recycling collection point can sometimes be greater than that you save through the recycling itself.

What to do with the compost

You'll know the compost is ready to use when it's 'clean' and crumbly, looks like earth, and when it doesn't smell. If you have a small heap of your own, you can use the compost on the flower beds in the garden, or around the base of young trees, to help feed the roots and keep the weeds down. If you can set up a large-scale production line – perhaps a whole series of compost heaps to take the waste from school kitchens and canteens – then when the compost is ready you could put it in bags and sell it to gardeners. It's a good way of raising money for conservation.

There is a group of nature conservationists in New York who take the manure from the Bronx Zoo, compost it with other kinds of vegetable waste, and then sell it as 'Zoo-Doo'.

Testing biodegradability

As you're building your compost heap, you might like to try an experiment. Include various kinds of waste, and see which of them will rot down, and which won't. Some things are obvious. A plastic bottle is non-biodegradable –

it'll look as good as new when you dig it up, but its paper label will probably have rotted away.

Other things may surprise you. Some plastic carrier bags are biodegradable – although the plastic actually just breaks down into tiny pieces. It doesn't actually decompose. Some wrappers that you might think are biodegradable paper turn out to be non-biodegradable plastic, and quite a lot of things are a mixture – disposable nappies for instance, are often part biodegradable paper or padding, and part plastic. Mixtures like that are very difficult to recycle – either on your compost heap or even back at the factory.

Compost heaps – summary

What you need

Timber to make the compost box, plus a saw, hammer and nails.
Get an adult to help with the hammering (why bash your thumb when theirs will do).
A piece of old carpet to make a lid.
Rubbish to rot down.

Where to compost

Close to the kitchen, but not too close as it can get a bit smelly.

When to start

Any time of year – but the compost heap works fastest in spring and summer.

How a compost heap helps reduce pollution locally

Recycles organic biodegradable waste naturally, and saves on bin lorry traffic and the filling up of holes in the ground.

How composting could help pollution nationally

One-third of all our rubbish could be composted. We spend millions of pounds taking it away and dumping it, and bin lorries travel millions of polluting miles each year carrying it for us.

Two compost heaps, each about the size of a fridge, will be enough to take all the organic waste produced by an average family, and turn it into compost. That means no more polluting garden fires, no more methane-rich biogas from your waste, and only half the amount of energy used in transporting rubbish to the tip. Not only that, but the compost can go back in the garden, grow better plants, improve the soil and help support all its resident wildlife. The compost will help save some of Britain's most important wetland nature reserves, too, because it is an excellent alternative to peat. The peat which gardeners buy in their grow-bags and potting compost is dug up from rare peat bogs out in the countryside.

Compost heaps can also work on a big scale. They don't have to be restricted to a gloomy corner of the garden. School and office canteens can produce mountains of vegetable waste that could be composted, and parks departments should be composting their leaf-sweepings and lawn clippings too. The city of Zurich, in Switzerland, has set up a compost campaign. Hundreds of local groups have made joint compost heaps in their neighbourhoods, and there is even a telephone 'compost hotline' to help people who want to reduce pollution this way.

Now, giant compost heaps are being built here in Britain. A company in Cambridgeshire has found a way of making money out of the pollution problem. They take straw from the farmers – saving the environment from polluting straw-burning; they take tankers of liquid sewage from the sewage works – saving the streams and rivers from water pollution; and they mix the two magic ingredients together, using big machines to move the heaps around. This makes sure they contain plenty of life-giving air, and the micro-organisms do the rest. As they work away they make the heaps incredibly hot and steamy. Within two weeks the waste straw and the waste sewage have been transformed into a sweet-smelling compost, ready to go back into the land as fertilizer.

Encouraging the wildlife clean-up brigade

Giant reeds, green slime and creepy-crawlies aren't the only 'organisms' that can help prevent pollution by dealing with organic waste. In fact, by encouraging wildlife generally, we make the landscape richer and more varied, and that tends to encourage more of the wildlife we describe as *scavengers* – the creatures who clean up anything edible. In the plains of Africa it is the vultures who swoop in for the pickings, but here in Britain we have our own clean-up brigade, and some of the animals concerned are pretty spectacular themselves.

Just think how much biodegradable rubbish is dropped in our city streets each day. Some of it is swept up by the street-cleaners, of course, but a lot of the rest disappears mysteriously under cover of darkness. Cats and urban foxes do most of the work. Foxes will hide all day in the safety of an overgrown churchyard, or under the brambles on the railway embank-ment, and as the last late-night bus leaves town, they trot out of their hiding places to start the job of 'scavenging'.

Wild foxes are doing very well in our towns and cities, but they could do even better. They depend on access to water, as well as food, so garden ponds are important. They also need plenty of cover in the daytime, so the wilder corners of town are really valuable to them. All too often these places are tidied up, with the result that the wildlife is driven out, and the foxy clean-up brigade have to move on.

Foxes aren't the only urban scavengers, though they're probably the most spectacular. The humble town pigeons also do a thoroughly good job, pecking away at almost anything they can find. Starlings, too, will tackle most things, and over 30 million of them fly from Russia and Scandinavia each autumn to spend the winter months in Britain. That's quite an army of rubbish pickers, and when you see them rummaging around in the litter-bins, it's obvious that almost anything edible will be snapped up pretty quickly. Everywhere you look you can see the wildlife clean-up brigade, busy doing their job. Crows and magpies patrol the roadside verges, waiting for traffic victims. Black-headed gulls seem almost to have abandoned the sea and now commute between their standing roosts on sports pitches, and their banqueting grounds at the rubbish tips.

There is one group of wildlife scavenger that deserves a special mention: those that feed in the mud of our coastal estuaries. The organic pollution that flows from our farms and sewage works travels down the rivers, or is pumped directly to the sea. Much of that pollution comes to rest on the beaches, and particularly on the tidal mud-flats at the mouth of each river. Tidal estuaries are the winter feeding ground for millions of wild migratory birds. Waders and ducks fly here from Greenland, Iceland, Scandinavia, and even as far afield as Canada and Siberia. These great flocks of birds feed on the waste that collects in the mud, or on the small creatures – shellfish, worms, etc. – that themselves make use of this pollution. Waders such as dunlin, redshank and turnstone poke their bills down into the soft mud, while shelduck feed by sucking mud through their bills, and sifting out tiny snails. All this super-efficient feeding removes a great deal of organic waste from the mud system before it can reach the sea beyond. To do the job by artificial means would be very expensive, and probably no more efficient, and yet over half Britain's estuaries are under threat. There are plans to build dams across several of them to trap the river water, and stop the tide going up and down. If these schemes go ahead, the waders will be left homeless, and the levels of pollution in the rivers will rise, so the conservationists who campaign to save wader habitat are also helping in the fight against pollution.

6 Reducing Waste and Re-Using It

Probably the most interesting and effective way of reducing pollution at a personal level is to tackle the throw-away society. Save old or worn out things from being dumped and find new uses for them. That's a great contribution to pollution control.

You're probably doing a lot already. Second-hand things are often taken for granted. The clothes handed down from older brothers and sisters, for instance, strike an important blow for the environment. Jumble sales are really brilliant recycling events, and it's amazing how something you can't stand the sight of for a moment longer always turns out to be exactly what someone else is looking for. If jumble sales aren't quite your scene, then you might prefer to buy your 'nearly new' spring collection from the Oxfam shop, or a car-boot sale, or if you're really posh you'll no doubt prefer an antiques emporium. They're all the same thing, really – places to buy things that other people don't want anymore, to save them from being dumped.

In Germany and Holland, the children have a really good recycling tradition. Several times a year, on particular days – usually at weekends – the streets or parks are turned into second-hand toy markets. There are no adults involved, just hundreds of young traders, covering their picnic tables or blankets with books, toys, games and anything else that they've been given in the past, and don't want anymore. Some of the stuff is sold for cash, but a lot of the deals are done by swapping one thing for another. At the end of the day thousands of items have changed hands. They've all got proud new owners who presumably get a whole lot of fresh enjoyment out of them, and if boredom eventually sets in, then the goodies can always be traded in at the next children's toy fair.

Re-using things for the same purpose over and over again is easy. What is much more difficult is to find different new uses for old things. Giving an old pram a new lease of life by turning the wheels into a racing-trolley, or taking the electric pump out of an old washing machine, and using it to run a fountain in the back garden – that's much more challenging.

The people in third world countries are brilliant at adapting things that we would simply throw away. When car tyres are too badly worn to drive on, they are cut up and turned into sandals. Whole houses are made from recycled packing cases, and even musical instruments are made out of rubbish. A West Indian steel band must be one of the most wonderful examples of re-use – all that music coming from old oil drums. In some communities nothing is wasted, and that really is a lesson we have to learn in wasteful western countries, too.

In industry, waste costs money, so conservation, recycling and re-use are becoming an important part of good business management. Containers are the obvious examples. It would be very easy for a manufacturer just to send out products in throw-away containers, and build the cost into the price. Of course, lots of them do – just think of all those washing machines and fridges in their cardboard and polystyrene boxes – but there are companies that make an effort to re-use their containers.

Some bakers, for instance, delivery their bread and cakes to the shops on plastic or metal trays, and use them over and over again, collecting one day's trays when they make the next day's delivery.

Dairies deliver their milk in glass bottles that we wash and put out on the step for collection when they're empty, so they get used many times over. That saves the pollution that would be caused by dumping them, and the energy involved in making new ones. Pubs do the same. Their bottled beer and soft drinks are delivered from the brewery in returnable bottles, and the lorry takes away the crates of empties each time a new delivery arrives.

There are plenty of signs that industry is starting to 'go green' and tackle pollution by reducing their use of energy, by using materials more wisely, and by cleaning the waste products before they release them into the environment. Most begin with the easy things – collecting office waste-paper for recycling, and using recycled paper themselves for notepaper, reports, etc; cleaning the offices with polishes and sprays that are 'ozone-friendly', and don't contain polluting chemicals like CFCs; and converting the fleet of company cars to run on unleaded petrol.

It takes much longer for them to change the way they run the company or manufacture their product, but many of them are at least starting to try.

Action in industry

To give some idea of the way industry is beginning to tackle pollution, it's worth a brief look at the car-makers. The cars themselves are basically very bad for the environment: probably our most serious source of pollution. The practice of constantly bringing out 'new models' each year is wasteful, too. It tends to encourage people to sell their cars long before they're worn out, although of course they are recycled through second-hand car dealers.

Since most cars spend a great deal of time crawling through slow-moving heavy traffic, the fashion for big engines with more power than they can use is very wasteful, too, and unnecessarily polluting. However, there have been a number of interesting refinements in manufacture, aimed partly at reducing environmental damage.

First, small cars are much comfortable than they used to be, so it's no longer necessary to 'buy big' in order to buy safety or comfort. The most positive thing any car owner can do to help reduce environmental damage is to buy a smaller car with a smaller engine, using less fuel, and made from fewer raw materials.

The car-making process itself uses a huge amount of energy, and the more mechanised it becomes, with conveyor belts and robots, the more emphasis there is likely to be on using electricity. All that moving around and lighting of the production line produces a lot of wasted heat – or at least in most factories it's wasted. On Volvo's new production line, in Sweden, they collect all that heat, and instead of just wasting it, they re-circulate it to heat the offices and the factory itself. Sainsburys are doing much the same thing in their most modern supermarkets – capturing the heat that is produced out of the back of all their freezers and cooling cabinets, and using it to heat their offices and shop. That's saving energy and so reducing pollution, but it was also saving about £40,000 in heating bills in an average store in 1989.

One of the most polluting stages in car manufacturing is the painting of the bodywork. The smell you get from fresh paint is actually the smell of the chemicals used to carry the colour. Once the paint is sprayed or dipped onto the body-work, it dries, and releases the chemical solvent into the air. This is a very serious pollutant, containing some of the chemicals that are helping to cause the hole in the ozone layer and the Greenhouse Effect. Now, there are modern paints available which Volvo and one or two of the other manufacturers are using, which don't contain the chemical solvent. Instead, the colour is mixed with good old-fashioned water – so now, when the paint is drying it is just water that evaporates. As a result, there's no smell, and no pollution either.

One very wasteful feature of modern cars is the way a small fault involves replacement of a big part. If a headlight fails, for instance, it's often impossible just to replace a little light bulb. The headlamp is designed as a sealed unit, and you have to throw the whole thing away and start again. If there's a noisy little 1cm hole in the exhaust pipe, it may be necessary to replace the whole exhaust system.

The garages and insurance companies make things worse than they need to be. If a car is damaged in an accident, and a bumper is dented, or there's a scratch on the paint work, then if the insurance company is paying, all the parts involved will be replaced with brand new ones. Now at last one or two of the manufacturers are identifying those parts of their cars that can be repaired, or dismantled and only partially replaced.

Of course this is exactly what all those little back-street motor-repair workshops in the scruffier parts of town have been doing for years: making up spares, welding bits and pieces together, and generally re-using and recycling almost anything the customer wants.

In the world of second-hand cars, even the engine and gear-box can be repaired and re-used. To do this properly, all the old oil and dirt has to be removed, and here again there have been environmental improvements. The normal way to carry out the cleaning is to wash the engine in a chemical solvent – something powerful that will dissolve all the gunge. Unfortunately, this then results in a pretty evil liquid which may finish up polluting a stream somewhere. Now, instead of using a solvent, it is possible to blast the old oil and dirt off the engine by spraying it with a jet of very hard steel balls. They're tiny, and very effective if the pressure is great enough.

What's clever about this new system is that the steels balls can then be picked up by a magnet, so the filthy mixture of gunge and steel balls is easily separated. The steel cleaning balls can be re-used over and over again. There's no expensive solvent to buy, and there is much less polluting waste to get rid of.

Motor manufacturers certainly aren't the only industrialists who are tackling waste and pollution. Here are some other examples:

- A sweet factory in Sheffield used to produce a great deal of sugary waste in their factory by the River Don. The waste was pumped into the water, and added to the river's pollution problems. When a new managing director took over, he realised this was both an environmental problem and a waste of something that could be useful. Now, they recycle all that waste. It saves them thousands of pounds a year, reduces pollution in the river, and presumably makes their sweets just a little bit cheaper than they would be if the original waste was still being thrown away.
- Bulmers had a similar problem. Millions of apples are crushed every year at their cider mill in Hereford, to produce the juice that they turn into delicious cider. Millions of squashed apples means tens of millions of apple pips – a mountain of waste that was very difficult to get rid of.

    There is a chemical in apple-pips, called pectin. It is used to help set jams more easily, and jam-makers buy pectin to add to other fruit. Now, instead of just crushing the apples, taking the juice and throwing the pips away, Bulmers extract the pectin from the pips, and the company has created a whole new business from their waste.
- Beer is made from hops, barley and water. When the brewer has extracted the flavour from the hops and barley, there's a massive amount of 'spent hops' left behind, and in the past that has often been given away to gardeners as a cheap organic material to dig into their soil – a very environmentally

friendly way of avoiding pollution. One brewery in North Wales has gone one stage further with its spent hops. It stores them in tanks, called digesters, and the hops decompose, giving off the same kind of biogas that is produced in rubbish-tips. The brewery uses this gas as a fuel, to heat its buildings, boil up its brewing beer, and even to generate its own electricity. After all the energy has been released from the hops, they're still marvellous as a manure for the local gardeners, the brewery is saving a lot on fuel bills, and it's not having to burn fossil fuels or power-station electricity, so it's cutting its pollution problem.

• Some farmers are starting to do the same kind of thing with manure from their cows, pigs or chickens. When animals are kept in buildings, or crowded together on concrete-floored yards, the build up of their dung, or slurry, can become a really serious environmental problem. The liquid that runs out of the slurry is a major cause of pollution in streams and rivers. In the past, the animals would have spent much more time out in the fields, and the manure would have been spread naturally by the animals themselves, but nowadays the food is brought to the cows, and there is usually much more manure than the farmer's own fields can take.

• At the Bethlehem monastery, in Northern Ireland, the monks put all the manure from their farm into a big digester. This produces enough biogas to heat their hospital and the rest of the monastery buildings, and they can still use the 'de-gassed' manure on the land.

• In some villages in Denmark, cow manure is collected from all the farms in the neighbourhood, brought by tanker to a central depot, and used to produce biogas to heat the surrounding houses.

This kind of solution, where a waste material is recycled to produce something really useful, must be the best way of dealing with pollution.

Recycling materials

It obviously isn't possible to re-use everything over and over again. Some things are designed to be used only once. A drinks can, for instance, has to be air-tight. When you pull the ring, you hear the hissing sound of the fizz escaping; the seal is broken, and you can't re-seal it.

You can put the screw top back on a bottle, so it can be emptied and filled many times over, but it will be difficult to make it truly air-tight again without sending it back to the manufacturer.

Newspapers are obviously pretty useless after they've been read – unless you use them to wrap up fish and chips, stuff inside wet shoes to help them to dry, cut them up for hamster bedding or find some other secondary use.

Plastic yoghurt pots are easy to find new re-uses for – just watch Blue-Peter if you want ideas – but there is a limit to the number of seedling pots, pencil holders and do-it-yourself tooth-mugs that a yoghurt-eater can use, and pretty soon you're throwing the pots away.

All these throw away things, and many more besides, are manufactured using raw materials and energy. The glass in bottles, for instance, is made by heating sand and limestone to very high temperatures. Drink cans are made from aluminium or steel, and these metals are produced by taking the natural rock – ironstone for steel, or bauxite for aluminium, and melting the metal out of it. Again there's a very high use of energy. Paper and cardboard is mostly made from trees, mashed to pulp in big machines, washed and rolled using masses of energy in the process. Most plastics are made from oil or coal – two raw materials we need to use very wisely, because eventually they will run out.

With all these things, and many more besides, it is possible through industrial processes to re-use some of the raw materials to make new products. We can melt down old glass bottles, make new glass and manufacture more bottles. We can re-pulp newspapers, clean out the ink of the newsprint, and make new paper. This is *recycling,* and obviously it saves the raw materials, and can reduce pollution too. Without recycling, many of these things would end up as litter, or as extra waste material in need of disposal.

Recycling can also help pollution in another way: through energy conservation! It takes 10 times as much energy to make an aluminium drink can from the ore-stone, bauxite, as it does if the manufacturer can start by melting down used aluminium cans. Less energy means less electricity. That usually means less burning or fossil fuels, so less polluting smoke.

There is yet another advantage in recycling. The raw materials, and the energy savings, are worth money to the manufacturers, so they may be prepared to pay for the old bottles, cans, paper and other recycleable things, provided they're collected in large quantities. A lot of WATCH groups make money for conservation by collecting waste, and selling it for recycling.

Glass is probably the material we have been recycling longest in Britain, and bottle-banks are now quite common. They are nearly all provided by local councils, and placed in convenient places such as supermarket car parks, where we bottle recyclers can drive in and empty our load. There is not really any scope for money-making by individuals here, although a lot of councils do give the money they earn from their glass-recycling bottle-bank to charity. Bottle-banks are very noisy – it's such fun, smashing the bottles when you drop them in – so they need to be sensible places where the sound of shattering glass won't disturb the neighbours.

Usually the bottle-banks come in families of three – one green, one brown and one clear – and if everyone takes the trouble to match the colour of the bottle to the colour of the container, then that makes it easier for the glass manufacturers to re-use the glass. A mixture of brown, green and clear broken glass means they can really only produce a dull coloured glass by recycling.

Careful separation is even more important in plastics recycling. There are lots of different kinds. Some are clear and hard, some are cloudy and soft. Some are very brittle, and crack easily, while others are bendy and unbreakable. For recycling, the plastics manufacturers really need the different types kept separate.

If clear fizzy-pop bottles can be collected on their own, for instance, then the plastic they're made of is quite easy to recycle, and that is well worth doing. Most carrier bags are made of one kind of plastic too, so they can be easily recycled. A whole mixture of different plastics makes life much more difficult for manufacturers.

One thing that manufacturers themselves are now starting to do is to make products and packaging which are designed to be easily recycled. The old style pop-bottles with a clear body and black base are disappearing, because the two kinds of plastic in each bottle immediately causes recycling problems. Some drinks cans used to be made from steel, but with aluminium ends. Now they're almost all either one thing or the other. The paper in magazines and books is difficult to recycle if the pages are stuck together with certain kinds of rubbery glues, so gradually the printers are switching to water-based glues that don't interfere with the re-pulping system.

Collecting and recycling waste material is obviously a good idea, but there is a catch. All those recycling environmentalists, driving to the bottle-banks in their cars, with clanking collections of bottles, can use up more energy and produce more pollution than the recycling itself is able to save. That is why it makes such good sense to collect on a very local level, and then make occasional major visits to the recycling centre.

Friends of the Earth, in Bristol, have an even better idea. They collect the waste paper direct from people's front doors, and to reduce pollution and energy use even further, they carry out their door-to-door collections with a horse and cart. There is still a little pollution of course, but it comes in little steaming heaps, and is easily recycled onto the nearest rose-bed.

Things you can do to cut down on waste

- Use less paper (write on both sides).
- Pass on used toys, clothes and other things you don't want any longer.
- Organise a jumble sale.
- Join in the family shopping, and steer the trolley away from over-packaged products, towards bigger more efficient packs, or unpacked products.
- Re-use the plastic carrier bags.
- Collect other people's waste paper.
- Drink tap water, and snack on fresh fruit instead of consuming canned and bottled drinks and packaged sweets.

Things you can do to recycle more waste

- Set up a collection service for taking bottles, paper, plastic, cans, etc. to the local recycling centre.
- Write to the local council asking for more recycling facilities. What about engine oil, the CFCs in fridges, and old clothes?
- Feed the birds in the garden on any suitable waste food.
- Take over responsibility for managing your family's compost heap.

7 Saving Energy to Reduce Pollution

Some of our worst pollution problems come from burning fossil fuels: coal, oil and gas. There are three main areas where we can cut down:

- We use a lot of energy in transport, so if we can be more efficient with that we will reduce pollution.
- We produce pollution when we burn fuel either to generate electricity, in power stations, or in central-heating boilers. Cutting down on the heat and power we use reduces the pollution we cause.
- Most of the manufactured products we use everyday are made using a great deal of energy, so when we buy a book like this, a bag of sweets, or something more elaborate such as a car or a washing machine, we're buying a lot of 'buried energy', and buried second-hand pollution, too.

The subject of energy conservation is a whole book in itself, and while there is a lot that individuals can do, much of the progress needs to come from manufacturers.

They are beginning to think about energy conservation much more than they used to: for instance, some washing machines are now labelled to show how much power they will take to run. However, far too many things are still being made to last only a short time, and many things have to be thrown away if they break down. They're not meant to be repaired.

Our whole economic system is based on a few big companies making most of the products. This tends to mean a great deal of transport bringing the materials together, and then re-distributing those products all around the country. Corn grown in the Midlands may well be loaded up and driven to a cornmill in the south, ground into flour and then transported to Scotland, baked into biscuits then driven down to the south again to be sold in the shops. If a family in London takes those biscuits on a picnic to Cornwall, you can see that they will have an enormous amount of energy 'buried' in them by the time they are eaten, and they will have been responsible for quite a lot of pollution, too.

Much of the buried energy we buy is in packaging and other 'throw-away' items, and this creates a double pollution problem. Not only are we polluting through the energy used in manufacture and transport, but the material itself often turns into polluting litter, or a waste-disposal problem. All those glass bottles, plastic wrappers, polystyrene packages, cardboard boxes, foil containers and tin cans together make up almost half the rubbish we throw away.

Of course, some of this packaging is very useful to us. Imagine buying your yoghurt loose, without the throw-away plastic pot. Manufacturers do need to reduce the amount of packaging they use, though, and if at the same time we all start avoiding unnecessary packaging, then we can turn a double pollution problem into a double improvement.

Traffic and transport

The motor car is a serious polluter, so anything we do to cut down on our car travel must be good for the environment. Any driver will know how all the rush-hour traffic jams seem to disappear as soon as the school holidays arrive. Millions of lazy children are driven to school each day by their parents and that really does clog up the roads for most of the year. If the traffic is slow, then each journey burns more fuel, and pushes out far more polluting exhaust gas. For short journeys to school or the shops, why not walk, roller-skate or cycle, and if parents are worried about the danger of that – especially from the traffic – suggest that they keep you company on their own bikes.

Buses and trains are much less environmentally damaging than cars. The individual vehicles may still produce pollution, but they carry so many more people. Millions travel to and from work each day, sitting one to a car in rush-hour traffic. Persuade the people you know to leave their cars behind. If they can't walk or cycle, they should take a bus or train. At the very least make sure that if they can't be parted from their precious cars, they share the journeys. In Los Angeles, companies are being forced to make it easier for employees to share a car to work, just as a way of speeding up traffic, and cutting down on pollution.

Nowadays it's possible for lots of people to work from home at least part of the time, and cut out polluting journeys altogether. The telephone and the fax machine can make a great contribution to pollution control by helping people work without needing to travel.

Energy conservation

Save energy, and you reduce pollution. For most of us, this is a matter of cutting down on the electricity we use in the home, or the amount of energy we use on heating. At its simplest level, switching off lights when they're not being used; using a desk lamp for reading instead of lighting a whole room; closing doors and windows to cut down the draughts; and not using both the television and the radio at the same time – those are the kind of everyday things that help. You might try wearing warmer clothes in winter, instead of just turning up the heating, and why not take a shower rather than a bath to use less hot water, and save energy that way.

The really efficient way to save energy in the house, or at schools, or in any other buildings, for that matter, is to insulate. We waste a large amount of energy just through 'leaky' buildings. The Department of Energy produces useful leaflets on saving energy in the home. The important thing to tell anyone who's going to make a start is that some insulation measures are more effective than others, and some give much better value for money. Top of the list is putting a cozy insulating jacket around the hot-water tank. That's cheap, and saves its cost in reduced bills inside six months. Most of the heat lost from a building travels out through the roof, because hot air rises, so the loft space under the roof should be really well insulated to keep in the heat. Most people have a 50mm layer of fibre-glass matting or something similar. That's a start, but it's not nearly enough. 150mm thickness is now considered the minimum needed to do the job properly.

A building will not be very energy efficient if there is a howling gale whistling under the doors and through gaps around the windows. Good draught-proofing is cheap and easy to do, and really is effective.

The windows let out a lot of heat, but if you have two layers of glass instead of one, the air trapped in between acts as insulation. That's the idea behind double-glazing, but proper double-glazing is very expensive, and it may involve throwing away the old windows. That doesn't match up to the kind of environmentally friendly projects we're trying to encourage. There is also a good deal of energy 'buried' in the specially made double-glazing units, and some of them are even made out of hardwood from the tropical rain forests. Something that is much more cost-effective than double-glazing is secondary glazing. Leave the old window in place, but fix another sheet of glass, or clear plastic, on the inside. At its cheapest you can do that with a sheet of polythene and some drawing pins, but that won't be clear enough to see through properly. Proper fixing clips and glass or clear perspex are much better, and not too expensive. They pay for themselves in energy saving in about three years. Drawing the curtains at night, especially if they're thick, is probably the most cost-effective measure of all.

The walls themselves do let out the heat, especially in older buildings. Most houses built since about 1950 have a double outer wall, with a central space or cavity. Again, the air space acts as an insulator. It can be made even more effective by filling the cavity with insulating foam, but there may be a pollution price to pay. Polystyrene foam used to be used, but if it's made using CFC gases, then in the manufacturing process it will have caused damage to the ozone layer. Now, though, there are friendlier foams available.

It's all very well keeping heat energy in, but it helps much more if we use less of it in the first place. A thermostat is a clever device for controlling the temperature, and usually central heating systems have just one of them, often on the wall in the living room. If that's all the control there is, then when it's comfortable in the living room it's probably too hot upstairs in the bedrooms, where the heat collects. With a thermostat on the radiator in each room, it's possible to control the use of energy much more carefully, and if you can lower the temperature in all the rooms and switch off completely in those that aren't being used, then that will save money, energy and pollution. A drop of 1°c is hardly noticeable, but it can save as much as 10 per cent of the energy you use.

Of course, electricity doesn't have to be generated in dirty power stations in the first place. We don't have to burn coal or oil to make it, or even depend on nuclear power, with all the risks that that involves. It is possible to capture natural energy, and either to use it directly – a conservatory captures the warmth of the sun, and helps the tomatoes grow – or use it to generate electricity. If we could capture more wind power, sun power, wave power and water power, then we could use it for all the energy-demanding luxuries we enjoy, without needing to worry about its effect on acid rain, holes in the ozone layer or the earth's climate.

Cutting back on chemicals

Look in the cleaning cupboard, or under the kitchen sink, or out in the garden shed or the garage. Most families use all kinds of chemicals. They are usually bought to help make the immediate environment cleaner and shinier: spray for the windows; disinfectant for the bathroom; scourers for the pots and pans; weedkillers and insecticides for the garden. All these chemicals end up in the wider environment, and some of them are very damaging indeed. It's usually possible to use less of most of these chemicals. In your fight against pollution that's a good way to begin.

Some chemicals are less damaging than others, so it's possible to choose 'environmentally friendly' washing powders, for instance, or use vinegar to clean the sink, instead of harmful bleach. Some chemicals can be dropped entirely – and that applies especially to all those pesticides that gardener's use. There are a million acres of gardens in Britain. They ought to be full of singing birds, with butterflies fluttering by, frogs swimming in the ponds, and hedgehogs snuffling through the vegetable patch on summer evenings. Instead, most gardens are treated like battlefields, where chemical warfare aims to wipe out pests, weeds and diseases. Until 50 years ago, gardeners managed perfectly well without any of the moss killers, fungicides, herbicides, insect sprays and slug pellets that they seem to think are essential today.

If gardens can be turned into pesticide-free zones, where

wildlife is welcomed instead of being wiped out, the gardeners would save a lot of time and money, most plants would grow just as well, and that would be one major source of chemical pollution we could wave goodbye to. In Europe, mainly in West Germany, entire towns have turned themselves 'pesticide-free', and the parks departments aren't allowed to use weed killer sprays anymore.

8 Saving the Planet Single-Handed

We just can't keep on polluting the earth more and more. We must stop treating the earth as a dustbin, imagining it can cope with anything we throw at it. Already there are signs that some of the land and the water is so damaged by the poisonous waste dumped in the past that it is unlikely ever to recover. It is convenient to think that when an oil tanker runs aground, a chemical works burns down or a nuclear power station blows up, it is nothing to do with us. The fact is that we are all guilty, each and everyone of us. The goods we buy, the electricity we take for granted, the transport that we travel in, and the waste that we carefully flush away – all these are combining to create the pollution problems we see all around us. Changes have to be made now. Everyday that we delay is a day lost, and already it is almost too late.

There are some pollution solutions that can only come from industry, but there are many ways in which individual people can reduce waste and pollution in their daily lives, and that's where you come in.

There are two ways that young people can help. One is to really change the way they live themselves, and the other is to persuade the older people around them to make changes.

There is no doubt that children have made a great impression on their parents and teachers as the green movement has developed. Nagging away about 'not spraying poisons on the garden' or 'not emptying paint cleaner down the sink' does get through eventually, though not getting washed so often, 'because of the damage the soap will do to the North Sea', is probably less likely to do the trick.

So start making changes now. Make sure you try to leave every day a little less polluted than you find it, and do whatever you can to make sure everyone you know joins in the fight against pollution. Together we can still help the earth to get better.

Glossary of Terms

Acid   A sour substance, able to corrode and dissolve, which turns litmus paper red.

Acid rain   Rain (or snow) with acid dissolved in it – mostly sulphuric acid from smoke and fumes. Dissolves some rocks, damages trees and pollutes streams.

Aeration   Process of introducing air, e.g. into sewage, compost or river water.

Alkali   A substance which turns litmus paper blue, and counters the affect of an acid.

Arable   Describes farmland that is ploughed up to grow crops.

Bacteria   Tiny organisms, only visible through a microscope. Neither plants nor animals. Some are important for decay in the soil. Other cause diseases.

Biogas   A fuel. A mixture of gases – mainly methane – produced naturally when manure and other organic wastes rot down without oxygen.

Biodegradable   Any substance that can be broken down naturally. Paper, wood, sewage and autumn leaves are all biodegradable. Plastic and glass are not.

Carbon dioxide   A natural gas produced when plants and animals 'breathe'. Also produced when fuels such as coal, oil, gas and wood are burned. Now increasing, and adding to the greenhouse effect.

Catalytic converter Fits into the exhaust pipe of a petrol-driven vehicle and reduces some of the pollution.

CFCs Chloroflourocarbons. A group of man-made gases that damage the ozone layer. Included in refrigerators and air conditioners. Also used in aerosols and to blow the bubbles into some polystyrene foams.

Compost A mixture of organic materials that have been rotted down by bacteria, worms, insects and fungi. Used to grow seedlings and young plants.

Decompose To rot down organic materials.

Energy The power to do work. Energy is stored in fuel, so burning coal or oil, for instance, releases its energy.

Energy conservation The saving of energy, using as little energy as possible.

Environment Everything that makes up our surroundings.

Fertilizer A chemical that promotes plant growth.

Fossil fuels Oil, coal and natural gas – the remains of plants, buried underground for millions of years, and non-renewable. Once we burn them for their energy, they are gone forever.

Germinate Start to grow. Seeds germinate, usually when they are given warmth, air and water.

Greenhouse effect A layer of gases, including carbon dioxide, form a kind of blanket high up in the sky, all around the earth. This layer helps keep in the heat of the sun, and as the gases get thicker – a result of burning fuels – more of the sun's heat is trapped, and the earth warms up.

Herbicide A man-made chemical weed killer.

Hibernation Where winters are cold, some animals hibernate. They hide away, they slow right down, as if they are deep asleep, and so conserve their energy till the warm weather of spring returns. Hedgehogs, bats and frogs all hibernate. Birds do not hibernate, but some migrate to warmer climates each year instead.

Invertebrates Small animals without backbones. Worms, slugs, snails and insects are all invertebrates.

Insulator A substance that keeps in heat (or electricity). Woolly jumpers insulate us from the cold.

Larva A grub or caterpillar. The stage in the life of an insect before it becomes an adult with wings.

Landfill Large holes in the ground, used for dumping our rubbish. Often produce Biogas as the rubbish rots down underground.

Manure Animal droppings (or compost) used by farmers and gardeners as fertilizer on the soil.

Migrate Some species of animals travel along fixed routes, at regular times, e.g. swallows and cuckoos migrate from Britain to Africa each autumn, and return in spring. Frogs migrate to their original pond each year to breed.

Nitrate A chemical needed for plants to grow. As a fertilizer it can wash through the soil, and cause pollution in streams and rivers.

NRA National Rivers Authority. The government organisation that controls the quality of our water.

Organic Anything that is, or has been living; all plants and animals. Also used to describe food produced by organic farming.

Organic farming and gardening No use of man-made weed-killers, pesticides or fertilizer. Uses the natural fertility of the soil, the energy from the sun, and the balance of nature.

Organisms Individual plants or animals. Humans are organisms. So are eagles, slugs, cabbages and mushrooms.

Ozone A gas which helps protect the earth from the burning rays of the sun. At ground level produced partly from car exhaust fumes reacting with sunshine, and causing serious health problems.

Pesticide Used to kill pests such as mosquitoes, aphids and slugs.

Phosphate A chemical used as a fertilizer, but also used in washing powder and detergent. Can pollute streams and rivers.

Plastic A man-made substance that can be moulded under heat and pressure. Lots of different plastics. Non-biodegradable. Most made from oil.

pH A measure of acidity and alkalinity. Below pH7 is acid, above pH7 is alkaline. pH7 is neutral.

Recycle To re-use the basic material in something that is no longer needed – e.g. recycling the glass in used bottles; recycling the aluminium in drinks cans; recycling the organic matter in vegetable peelings, by composting.

Refuse Garbage, junk. Things that are no longer any use to us.

Re-use To find a further use for something, e.g. yoghurt pot for growing plants; a plastic pop-bottle as a mini greenhouse.

Sewage Human waste, flushed down the lavatory, mixed with water, for treatment at the sewage works. Untreated sewage pollutes rivers, seas, and bathing beaches – and it smells.

Slurry A thin watery mixture of liquid with solid bits floating in it, e.g. cow manure and water; coal dust or mud and water. Can flow downhill, or be pumped through pipes.

Solvent A liquid that can dissolve other substances. Water is a solvent for sugar and salt. Polluting chemical solvents are usually made from oil or coal. You can smell the solvent when you use some glues, felt pens and paints.

Vertebrates Animals with backbones: mammals, birds, reptiles, fish and amphibians are all vertebrates.

Waste Anything that no longer has a use.

Further Information

Useful addresses

Acid Rain Information Centre
Department of Environment
and Geographical Studies
Manchester Polytechnic
Chester Street
Manchester M7 5GD
061–247 2000

Association for the Protection of Rural Scotland
14 Napier Road
Edinburgh EH10 5AY
031–229 1081

British Association of Young Scientists (BAYS)
BAAS
Fortress House
23 Savile Row
London W1X 1AB
071–494 3326

British Butterfly Conservation Society (BBCS)
Tudor House
Quorn
Leics LE12 8AD
0509–412870

British Plastics Federation
5 Belgrave Square
London SW1X 8PH
071–235 9896
Represents the major plastics
manufacturers, and provides
information on packaging,
recycling of plastics, and
plastic waste as fuel.

British Scrap Federation
16 High Street
Bramptom
Huntingdon
Cambs PE18 8TU
0430-55249
National federation of metal
recycling companies.

**British Trust for
Conservation Volunteers
(BTCV)**
36 St Mary's Street
Wallingford
Oxon OX10 OEU
0491-39766

**British Waste Paper
Association**
Highgate House
214 High Street
Guildford GU1 3JB
Can provide information on
paper recycling, local dealers,
paper container
manufacturers, etc.

**Can-Makers Recycling
Information Service**
36 Grosvenor Gardens
London SW1W OED

**Centre for Alternative
Technology (CAT)**
Llwyngwern Quarry
MacLynileth
Powys

Wales SY20 9AZ
0654-702400
Fax 0654-702782
Produces a book list and
other materials and provides
advice on energy and
alternative technology.

Common Ground
45 Shelton Street
London WC2H 9HJ
071-379 3109
A small limited company and
charity which promotes the
importance of a common
cultural heritage of nature
and landscape, and forges
links between the arts and
conservation. Projects
include parish maps.

**Community Recyling
Opportunities Programme**
7 Burners Lane
Kiln Farm
Milton Keynes MK11 3HA
0908-562 466

Council for Environmental Education (CEE)
School of Education
University of Reading
London Road
Reading
Berks RG1 5AQ
0734–318921
Produces comprehensive lists of all kinds of environmental education resources.

Council for the Protection of Rural England (CPRE)
Warwick House
25 Buckingham Palace Road
London SW1W OPP
071–976 6433
Fax 071–976 6373

Council for the Protection of Rural Wales (CPRW)
Ty Gwyn
31 High Street
Welshpool
Powys SY21 7JP
0938–2525
Campaigning organisation concerned with all aspects of countryside conservation. Runs an annual Youth Conference open to all sixth-formers to discuss hypothetical planning applications.

Countryside Commission for Scotland
Battleby
Redgorton
Perth PH1 3EW
0738–27921 Fax 0738–30583
As from 1 April 1992, the functions of the separate Countryside Commission for Scotland and Nature Conservancy Council are to be combined. The new body is provisionally called the Scottish National Heritage Agency. Send for details of publications.

Countryside Council for Wales
Plas Penhros
Ffordd Penhros
Bangor
Gwynedd LL57 2LQ
0248–37044 Fax 0248–355782

Department of Energy
1 Palace Street
London SW1E 5HE
071–238 3000
Produces a range of materials for older children on energy sources. Organises touring display on potential of renewable resources. Booklets and free details available on request.

**Fauna and Flora
Preservation Society (FFPS)**
79–83 North Street
Brighton BN1 1ZA
0273-820445
The oldest international
conservation organisation in
the world. In the UK
specialises in species
protection, e.g. bats,
amphibia.

Field Studies Council (FSC)
Preston Montford
Montford Bridge
Shrewsbury SY4 1HW
0743-850674
Centres offer facilities for
parties, residential courses.
Provides useful publications,
including Aidgap keys.

**Federation of Resource
Centres (FORC)**
c/o Playworks
25 Bullivant Street
St Anns
Nottingham NG3 4AT
Collects non-toxic waste
from business and industry
for children's play. Network
of play resource centres and
scrapstores.

Forestry Commission
231 Corstorphine Road
Edinburgh EH12 7AT

031-334 0303
Provides free teachers' pack;
charges for other
publications.

Friends of the Earth (FOE)
26–28 Underwood Road
London N1 7JQ
071-490 1555
Fax 071-490 0881
Campaigns on environmental
issues including energy,
pollution, the countryside,
tropical rainforest, water and
toxics, recycling. Network of
280 local groups. Produces
publications.

**Glass Manufacturers'
Federation**
19 Portland Place
London W1N 4BH
071-580 6952
Members represent most of
the buyers of recycled glass.

Greenpeace
30–31 Islington Green
London N1 8XE
071-354 5100
International campaigning
organisation; direct action
protests backed by extensive
scientific studies.

Groundwork Foundation
Bennett's Court
6 Bennett's Hill
Birmingham B2 5ST
021–236 8565
The co-ordinating body for
the Groundwork Trusts
which aim to bring together
the statutory, voluntary and
commercial sectors to carry
out environmental
improvements in and around
urban areas. Useful if there is
a trust in your area.

**Henry Double-Day Research
Association**
Ryton Gardens
Ryton on Dunsmore
Rugby
Warwicks
Organic gardening experts.

**Her Majesty's Inspectorate of
Pollution**
Department of the
Environment
Romney House
43 Marsham Street
London SW1P 3PY
071–276 8642
Fax 071–276 0818

Institute for Earth Education
Ian Duckworth Ufton
Court Centre
Green Lane
Ufton Nervet
Nr Reading
Berks RG7 4HP
An organisation dedicated to
improving people's
understanding of the natural
world by devising and
developing a range of
activities and programmes
carefully designed for
particular groups and
specific situations. Materials
are expensive but good. Send
SAE for catalogue. Produces
publications.

Mammal Society
Mammal Society Office
Department of Zoology
University of Bristol
Woodland Road
Bristol BS8 1UG
0272–272300
Fax 0272–732657
Produces publications on
small mammals, trapping,
owl pellets, etc. Excellent
series of small booklets on
common UK species. Free
factsheets for youth
members.

Marine Conservation Society (MCS)
9 Gloucester Road
Ross-on-Wye
Herefordshire HR9 5BU
0989–66017 Fax 0989–67815
Concerned with seashore and sublittoral marine conservation. Produces books, posters, etc. on marine wildlife.

National Association for Environmental Education (NAEE)
Wallsall Campus
Wolverhampton Polytechnic
Walsall WS1 3BD
0922–31200
Publishes a wide range of practical guides for environmental teaching, plus a newsletter and journal for members.

National Federation of City Farms
Avon Environmental Centre
Junction Road
Brislington
Bristol BS4 3JP
0272–719109
Send for details of publications and farms to visit.

National Rivers Authority
30–34 Albert Embankment
London SE1 7TL
071–820 0101
Fax 071–820 1603
(or look up the National Rivers Authority – Pollution Incidents Department)

National Society for Clean Air and Environmental Protection
136 North Street
Brighton
East Sussex BN1 1RG
0273–26313 Fax 0273–735802
Publishes excellent packs on pollution and leaflets.

Nature Conservancy Council for England
Northminster House
Northminster
Peterborough PE1 1UA
0733–340345 Fax 0733–68834
The statutory nature conservancy agency. Produces a few free or inexpensive leaflets. Free catalogue of publications available.

Nature Conservancy Council for Scotland
12 Hope Terrace
Edinburgh EH9 2AS
031–447 4784
Fax 031–447 0055
In 1992, the Countryside Commission for Scotland will merge with the Nature Conservancy Council for Scotland to form the Scottish Natural Heritage.

Northern Ireland 2000
Armagh House
Ormeau Road
Belfast B72 8HB
0232–238532
An umbrella organisation linking the voluntary environmental organisations with industrialists in the provinces. Kitemarks model environmental projects.

Reclamation Co-ordination Unit
Department of Trade and Industry
Ashdown House
123 Victoria Street
London SW1E 6RB
071–212 7676
Government department responsible for promoting waste reduction and recycling in industry.

Royal Society for Nature Conservation (RSNC)
The Green
Witham Park
Lincoln
Lincs LN5 7JR
0522–544400
Fax 0522–511616
National association for 48 Wildlife Trusts and umbrella body for ever 50 Urban Wildlife Groups. Produces publications.

Royal Society for the Prevention of Cruelty to Animals (RSPCA)
The Causeway
Horsham
Sussex RH12 1HG
0403–64181 Fax 0403–41048
Produces booklets on wildlife and animal care. Organises youth group. Videos on free loan.

Royal Society for the Protection of Birds (RSPB)
The Lodge
Sandy
Beds SG19 2DL
0767–680551
Junior club is Young
Ornithologists' Club.
Produces lists of school and
project ideas on birds.

Scottish Conservation Projects Trust (SCPT)
Baslallan House
24 Allan Park
Stirling FK8 2QG
0786–79697

Soil Association
Colston Street
Bristol BS1 5BB
0272–290661
Fax 0272–252504
Produces useful booklets
about organic gardening,
compost making, etc.

Tidy Britain Group (TBG)
The Pier
Wigan WN3 4EX
Has curriculum-related
programme on litter
prevention, including a
teachers' kit.

Tree Council
35 Belgrave Square
London SW1X 8QN
071–235 8854
Fax 071–235 2033
Promotes National Tree
Week each year in the
autumn. Tree species poster.
Gives small grants for school
tree-planting projects.

Trust for Urban Ecology (TRUE)
Stave Hill Ecological Park
Timber Pond Road
London SE16 1AG
071–237 9165
The trust brings nature into
the city by transforming
wasteland into nature parks,
as well as providing advice.
Produces publications for
landscape professionals and
for environmental education.

Waste Watch
National Council for
Voluntary Organisations
26 Bedford Square
London WC1B 3HU
071–636 4066
Fax 071–436 3188
National agency for the
promotion of recycling.
Provides advice and
information on all aspects of
recycling and reclamation.

**Watch Trust for
Environmental Education
(WATCH)**
The Green
Witham Park
Lincoln LN5 7JR
0522–544400
Fax 0522–511616
Runs a national
environmental club for
young people, organises
national projects and
promotes local clubs.
Produces publications.

Wildfowl and Wetlands Trust
Slimbridge
Glos GL2 7BT
0453–890333
Works for the conservation
of wildfowl and their wetland
habitats. Runs several
regional visitor centres. List
of publications available
from Education Department.

Wildlife Hospital Trust
1 Pemberton Close
Aylesbury
Bucks HP21 7NY
0296–29860 Fax 0296–437373
Treats sick or injured wild
birds and animals.

Woodland Trust
Autumn Park
Grantham
Lincs NG31 6LL
0476–74297
Mainly concerned with the
purchase and protection of
native deciduous woodland.
Keen to involve children in
tree-planting locally.
Produces education pack and
posters.

**WWF–UK (World Wide Fund
for Nature)**
Education Department
Panda House
Weyside Park
Godalming
Surrey GU7 1XR
0483–42644 Fax 0483–426409
Has an excellent education
programme which is a
response to the World
Conservation Strategy. Also
produces a free pack listing
its resources which include
music and drama and other
cross-curricular approaches.

Other resources

Here is a small selection from the mass of material available. Use your local library to borrow books and videos. That way you will be helping to recycle the information. Always look to see who has produced the leaflet, book or video you are using. If you want to understand the issues, you need to hear and see as many points of view as possible. A company which manufactures pesticides will give you different information from an organisation representing nature conservation. Road builders and car-makers will only give you one side of the traffic pollution story. Companies which sell bags of peat are hardly likely to be enthusiastic about home-made compost. Everywhere you look, there is information about pollution. This reference list should help answer any questions that arise as you investigate your local environment.

The list has been compiled with the help of the Council for Environmental Education.

General information

Books for parents and teachers
Baines, C. *How to Make a Wild Life Garden*, Elm Tree, 1986.
Baines, C. *The Wild Side of Town*, BBC, 1986.
Barwise, J. *Recycling: A Practical Guide*, Waste Watch (see page 121), 1991.
Bishop, O. *Adventures with Small Plants*, John Murray, 1983.
Carson, Rachel. *Silent Spring*, reissued by Fawcett (US), 1981. A classic work on pollution caused by pesticides and chemicals.
Gittins, Michael, J. *Pollution*, National Society for Clean Air, 1983. A guide to the types of pollution.
Hill, F. *Wild Life Gardening: A Practical Handbook*, Derbyshire Wildlife Trust, Elvaston Castle, Derby DE1 3EP, 1988.

Mossman, K. *Pip Book*, Penguin, 1977.

North, R. *The Real Cost*, Chatto, 1986. Explains the ways in which we, as consumers of certain products, affect the environment.

Owen, G. and Gordon, J. *Campaigning for Recycling: Ideas for Local Groups*, Waste Watch (see page 121), 1989.

Porritt, J. *Seeing Green: Politics of Ecology Supplied*, Basil Blackwell, 1984. A book about 'Green' politics. Readable and stimulating.

Rosenbaum, M. *Children and the Environment: How Pollution Puts Children at Risk*, Children's Legal Centre. 1989. An information sheet which examines the major pollution hazards to children; what action is being taken; and the framework of environmental law in Britain and Europe.

Seymour, J. and Girardet, H. *Blueprint for a Small Planet*, Dorling Kindersley, 1988. Describes how to take practical action to fight pollution.

Teaching packs and games

Harris Pollution Study Packs, Philip Harris Ltd, Oldmixon, Weston-Super-Mare, Avon BS24 9BJ. These 'five-student' packs are designed as an introduction to pollution studies and are useful for students of all ages. They contain illustrated background notes, survey forms and identification charts.

Pollution Game, Griffin and George, Bishop Meadow Road, Loughborough, Leics LE11 0RG. A game which simulates a pollution incident and the measures taken to control it. Students assume the role of industries, businesses and pollution control agencies. Approximate playing time is one hour. For 4 players or teams, aged 12 to adult.

Slick! A Conservation Game, BP Educational Service, PO Box 30, Blacknest Road, Blacknest, Alton, Hants GU34 4BR; BBC 40 track; BBC 80 track; Apple II. A computer programme introducing students to the problems of dealing with oil spills on an environmentally sensitive coastline. For 11–16 year olds.

Books for use with primary/middle school pupils

Bright, M. *The Dying Sea*, Survival Series, Franklin Watts, 1988. Looks at the wildlife under threat because of humans' failure to protect the environment.

Lambert, D. *Pollution and Conservation*, Wayland, 1985. An illustrated information book for 8–12 year olds. Includes types of pollution and wildlife conservation.

Lee, B. *Waste and Pollution*, Blackwell Education, 1990. Part of a complete science programme for 5–16 year olds, this book is designed for the 10–11 age range. Covers topics in National Curriculum Attainment Targets.

Films and Videos

Pollution – Who Cares? British Gas Film and Video Library, Park Hall Trading Estate, London SE21 8EL, 1988, 20 minutes. Shows how everyone has a personal responsibility for preventing pollution, and how popular protest and concern have led to changes.

Wallcharts and posters

Pollution, WWF-UK (World Wide Fund for Nature), Panda House Weyside Park, Godalming GU7 1XR, 1984. A colour wallchart and information sheet on pollution.

Air Pollution; Sea Pollution; River Pollution; Land Pollution, Pictorial Charts Educational Trust, 27 Kirchen Road, London W13 OUD. Four charts illustrating the causes and effects of pollution and showing how natural cycles are interrupted by pollutants.

Books for young people

Conserving Our World Series, Wayland, 1989/90/91. A series
   focusing on topical environmental issues. Titles include
   *Conserving the Atmosphere, Waste and Recyling, Protecting
   the Oceans, Farming and the Environment,* and *Conserving
   Our World.* For 10–16 year olds.
Elkington, J. and Hailes, J. *Young Green Consumer Guide.*
   Gollancz, 1990. Shows how young people, in their everyday
   acts and purchases, can reduce pollution and help the planet.
Hawkes, N. *Toxic Waste and Recycling,* Issues Series, Franklin
   Watts, 1988. Discusses the problems of waste disposal and
   who should be responsible for pollution control. For 11–16
   year olds.
Simon. *Pollution and Wild Life,* Survival Series, Franklin Watts,
   1987. Presents the threats to wildlife from pollution. For
   upper primary/lower secondary school children.

Acid rain

Books for pupils

Baines, J. *Acid Rain,* Conserving Our World Series, Wayland,
   1989. Looks at acid rain, its causes and effects and what is
   being done to prevent it. Includes case studies and practical
   activities. Aimed at 9–13 year olds.
Cochrane, J. *Water Ecology,* Project Ecology Series, Wayland,
   1987. An informative, activity-baed book which looks at how
   living things affect, and are affected by, the environment.

Films and videos

Acid Rain, Acacia Production, Team Video, 105 'Canalot', 222
   Kensal Road, London W10 5BN, 1986, 25 minutes. A three-
   part programme that examines the causes and environmental
   effects of acid rain across Europe.

Wallcharts
Acid Rain, Pictorial Charts Educational Trust, 27 Kirchen Road, London W13 OUD. Part of a series of full-colour charts which look at the causes and effects of pollution and show how natural cycles are interrupted by pollutants.

Air pollution

Teaching packs, games and software
Air Pollution Pack, National Society for Clean Air and Environmental Protection (see page 119), 1987. Explains pollution problems such as smog, lead, acid rain and the greenhouse effect, and suggests easy classroom experiments. Contains photocopiable fact sheets. For 9–11 year olds.

Films and videos
Air Pollution: A First Film, Viewtech Audio Visual Media, 161 Winchester Road, Brislington, Bristol BS4 3NJ, 12 minutes. A film for upper primary/lower secondary school level showing the results of air pollution and possible solutions for controlling it. Also from Viewtech, *The Earth: Its Atmosphere* (9 minutes), which discusses air movements and the effects of human activities on the structure of the atmosphere; suitable for secondary level.
The Sky is a Canvas, CFL Vision, PO Box 35, Wetherby, Yorks LS23 7EX, 1978, 22 minutes. Shows the duties of a clean air inspector interwoven with footage of Lowry paintings to demonstrate steps that have been taken to combat air pollution.

Wallcharts and posters
Lichens and Air Pollution, BP Education Service, PO Box 30, Blacknest Road, Blacknest, Alton, Hants GU34 4BR, 1982. A full colour wallchart for 12–16 year olds which illustrates

common and easily identifiable British species of lichen arranged in relation to a known air pollution resistance scale.

Chemical pollution

Note: includes pesticides and other toxic substances.

Reference material

Chemicals in the Community Leaflets, Chemical Industries Association, Kings Buildings, Smith Square, London SW1P 3JJ. A series of leaflets giving information on the chemical industry, the benefits it brings and possible hazards.

Dudley, N. *This Poisoned Earth: The Truth about Pesticides,* Piatkus Books, 1987. Looks at the dangers and political implications of pesticide use with reference to the Seveso and Bhopal disasters.

Pesticides Briefing Sheet, Friends of the Earth (see page 117). Provides facts on chemical pesticides, their effects on our health, wildlife and the countryside. Recommends alternatives.

Points of View Leaflets, Environmental Education Section, Nature Conservancy Council for England (see page 119). Aimed at teachers and senior students, this series is designed to give a balanced introduction to current controversial issues and to give basic facts and figures as well as different points of view. Titles include 'Nitrates', 'Insecticides', 'Herbicides' and 'Coastal Toxic Waste'.

Teaching material and material for pupils

Hawkes, N. *Toxic Waste and Recycling,* Issues Series, Franklin Watts, 1988. Part of a series for lower secondary school level which examines world issues. Looks at industrial and domestic waste as well as recycling.

Films and videos

Chemicals and the Environment, Chemical Industries Association, Kings Building, Smith Square, London SW1P 3JJ, 1986, 16 minutes. A video which explains how chemical waste is disposed of or recycled and shows how industry safeguards the environment.

The Ecology of Agriculture, Viewtech Audio Visual Media, 161 Winchester Road, Brislington, Bristol BS4 3NJ, 15 minutes. Examines the consequences of modern agricultural methods on plant and animal life including the effects of artificial fertilizers and insecticides.

Just Like Rain, Picture of Health Series, Concord Film and Video Council, 201 Felixstowe Road, Ipswich, Suffolk IP3 9BJ. Looks at the relationship between health and the use of pesticides.

Lead pollution

Films and videos

Concerning Swans, RSPB Video Hire Library, The Lodge, Sandy, Beds SG19 2DL, 1985, 28 minutes. A video which shows the swan's historial connection with humans and looks at the danger of pollutants, especially lead.

Water pollution

Material suitable for use by pupils

Cochrane. *Water Ecology,* Project Ecology Series, Wayland, 1987. Looks at humans' relationship with and impact on the environment. Contains information and experiments. For a reading age of 10+.

Films and videos

How Green is our Valley? Concord Films Council, 201 Felixstowe

Road, Ipswich IP3 9BJ, 1988, 26 minutes. Looks at the pollution of rivers from farm waste and sewage, focusing on the Thames Valley and the North Sea.

Protecting Our Rivers, Acacia Productions, Team Video, 105 'Canalot', 222 Kensal Road, London W10 5BN, 25 minutes. Looks at the pressures that rivers are under in both rural and urban environments.

Posters and wallcharts

Rivers Pollution, Sea Pollution, Pictorial Charts Educational Trust, 27 Kirchen Road, London W13 OUD, 1988. Two colour charts which look at water pollution issues.